SWU-NAP- 015

UNIFORMS OF RUSSIAN ARMY DURING THE NAPOLEONIC WAR VOL.10

UNDER THE REIGN OF ALEXANDER I EMPEROR OF RUSSIA BETWEEN 1801 AND 1825
CAVALRY: CUIRASSIERS, DRAGOONS & HORSE-JÄGERS

From the Viskovatov's greatest work:
"Historical description of the clothing and arms of the Russian Army"

English translation by Mark Conrad

SOLDIERSHOP PUBLISHING

AUTHOR

Aleksandr Vasilevich Viskovatov born 22 April (4 May New Style) 1804, died 27 February (11 March) 1858 in St. Petersburg, Russian military historian. He graduated from the 1st Cadet Corps and served in the artillery, the hydrographic depot of the Naval Ministry, and then in the Department of Military Educational Institutions. He mainly studied historical artifacts and the histories of military units. Viskovatov's greatest work was the Historical Description of the Clothing and Arms of the Russian Army.

TRANSLATOR

Mark Conrad is an American historian with a great interest for all the Russian history.

PUBLISHING'S NOTE

NOTE ABOUT BOOK PRINTING BEFORE 1925

Title: **UNIFORMS OF RUSSIAN ARMY DURING THE NAPOLEONIC WAR VOL. 10**
Cavalry: Cuirassiers, Dragoons & Horse-Jägers
By A.V.Viskovatov. English translation by Mark Conrad. First edition December 2016
Cover & Art Design: Luca S. Cristini. Plates re-colorations by Anna Cristini
ISBN code: 978-88-93271677

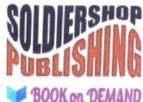

Published by Soldiershop publishing, via Padre Davide, 7 - 24050 Zanica (BG) ITALY. www.soldiershop.com

UNIFORMS
OF THE RUSSIAN
ARMY DURING THE
NAPOLEONIC WAR VOL.10

UNDER THE REIGN OF ALEXANDER I EMPEROR OF
RUSSIA BETWEEN 1801 AND 1825

*

Cavalry: Cuirassiers, Dragoons & Horse-Jäger

Portrait of a young Alexander I of Russia. Beginning of the 19th century

HISTORICAL DESCRIPTION OF THE CLOTHING AND ARMS
OF THE RUSSIAN ARMY - A.V. VISKOVATOV
(First English translation by Mark Conrad)

Soldiershop is glad to presents the complete collection of the great job made by A.V. Viskovatov dedicated to the uniforms and weapons belonging to the Russian army during the Napoleonic period, until 1825. The time we considered corresponds to the reigns of two Tzars: Paul I, who reigned since 1769 until his murder on the 23rd of March 1801, and his son Aleksandr Pavlovi☐ Romanov, that with the title of Alexander I, sat on the throne until the 1st December 1825.

Our reprint in based on the original 19th century volumes, to be precise the volumes from 7 to 9 are dedicated to the reign of Paul I; this first part is distributed on 7 volumes, having a numbering from 1 to 7. From number 10 to 18 of the original volumes, the second part is dedicated to the Russian troops under Alexander I. These still being worked on and they will be soon ready, distributed on twenty volumes approximately. Our new edition, the first ever published in English, both on paper and digital format, boasts a large number of color plates, many of them unpublished and coloured by our team of expert artists and scholars of uniformology. Each volume is based on 50/70 plates, always accompanied by the original translated text which describes the uniforms, the organization and the armament of the Russian army of the period.

A unique work in its genre, a must have in any respecting collection!

Aleksandr Vasilevich Viskovatov born 22 April (4 May New Style) 1804, died 27 February (11 March) 1858 in St. Petersburg, Russian military historian. He graduated from the 1st Cadet Corps and served in the artillery, the hydrographic depot of the Naval Ministry, and then in the Department of Military Educational Institutions.

He mainly studied historical artifacts and the histories of military units. Viskovatov's greatest work was the Historical Description of the Clothing and Arms of the Russian Army (Vols. 1-30, St. Petersburg, 1841-62; 2nd ed. Vols. 1-34, St. Petersburg - Novosibirsk - Leningrad, 1899-1948). This work is based on a great quantity of archival documents and contains four thousand colored illustrations.

Viskovatov was the author of Chronicles of the Russian Army (Books 1-20, St. Petersburg, 1834-42) and Chronicles of the Russian Imperial Army (Parts 1-7, St. Petersburg, 1852). He collected valuable material on the history of the Russian navy which went into A Short Overview of Russian Naval Campaigns and General Voyages to the End of the XVII Century (St. Petersburg, 1864; 2nd edition Moscow, 1946). Together with A.I. Mikhailovskii-Danilevskii he helped prepare and create the Military Gallery in the Winter Palace.

He wrote the historical military inscriptions for the walls of the Hall of St. George in the Great Palace of the Kremlin. (From the article in the Soviet Military Encyclopedia.)

CONTENTS

*

Russian Army: Cuirassiers, Dragoons, Horse-Jägers, 1801-1825

CHANGES IN THE CLOTHING AND ARMAMENTS OF ARMY CAVALRY, FROM 1801 THROUGH 1825:

I.   Cuirassier Regiments

II. Dragoon Regiments

III. Horse-Jäger Regiments

Notes.

I. CUIRASSIER REGIMENTS.

9 April 1801 — Lower ranks are ordered to cut off their **curls** [*pukli*] and have **queues** [*kosy*] only 7 inches [*4 vershka*] long, tying them midway down the collar (1).

9 August 1801— The **cuirasses** [*kirasy*] in Cuirassier regiments are withdrawn (2).

27 February 1802— In place of their previous **gloves** with gauntlets [*perchatki s kragenami*], officers of Cuirassier regiments are to have short gloves without gauntlets, of the pattern used at this time by infantry officers (3).

17 March 1802— Confirmation is given to the regulations for the cut, trim, and pattern of **Cuirassier uniforms**, for combatant as well as for noncombatant ranks (4).

30 April 1802— Confirmation is given to a new **table of uniforms, accouterments, and weapons of Cuirassier regiments**. Based on this table and the previously mentioned regulations, *cuirassier privates [ryadovye kirasiry]* are prescribed: *coat [kolet], pants [pantalony], jackboots [botfory], riding trousers [reituzy], boots [sapogi], neckcloth [galstuk], forage cap [furazhnaya shapka], smock [kitel], greatcoat [shinel], warm coat [fufaika], hat [shlyapa], gloves [perchatki], broadsword [palash] with swordknot [temlyak], swordbelt [portupeya], carbine [karabin] with sling [remen] and lock cover [ognivnyi chekhol], shoulder belt [pogonnaya perevyaz], cartridge pouch [lyadunka],* and when mounted — a pair of *pistols [pistolety]*. **Horse furniture and accessories** include: *saddle [sedlo] with saddle bucket [bushmat], holsters [olstredi], bridle [uzdechka], mouthpiece [mundshtuk], cruppers [pakhvi], chestband [papersti], saddle girth [podpruga], stirrups [stremena], cushion [podushka] for the pack load [vyuk], and small horse cloth [poponka]; shabrack [cheprak], pistol holder covers [chushki], valise [chemodan]. forage sack [furazhnyi sak], bag [torba], and water flask [vodonosnaya flyazha]* (5).

The ***coat*** is to be double-breasted, of white kersey [*kirza*], with a standing collar of a special color for each regiment. The cuffs, shoulder strap [*pogon*] (on the left shoulder), a light or piping [*proshiv ili vypushka*] at the sleeves' shoulder seams, and lining on the skirts and turnbacks, are all of the same color as the collar; with flat buttons that are yellow or white (tinned) in accordance with the distinctions listed below (Illus. 1401). This coat, in summer as well as winter, is ordered to be fastened with all its buttons, and the sizes of its parts, assuming a man 6 feet in height, are prescribed as follows:

Collar height, in front, at the edges — 3 1/2 inches, behind, at the middle — 4 inches; the upper edge shorter than the lower by 3 1/2 inches. Cuff (slit) width — 3 inches.

Length of the coat, from the collar to the waist — 17 1/2 inches, and from the waist to the ends of the skirts — 8 3/4 inches; width of the front turnover [i.e. the front breast part of the coat - M.C.] — 3 inches; distance of the first button from the collar — 1 inch; between the first and second buttons and so on — 2 5/8 inches; between the buttonholes and the edges of the turnover — 1/2 inch.

The lower edges of the coat [meaning the bottom of the tails - M.C.], remaining after the skirts are turned back — 4 inches, and the width of the trim [*vykladka*] on these turnbacks — 1 3/4 inches.

Length of the shoulder strap — 5 2/3 inches, its width at the shoulder — 1 3/4 inches, width at the button — 1 1/4 inches.

Buttons are sewn on in the following numbers: on each side of the front turnover — 6; on the collar, for the shoulder strap — 1; on the cuffs — 2 each; on the waist — 2; on the lower edges of the coat, where the skirt turnbacks meet — 1 at each point.

On the back of the coat, above the waist buttons, are sewn two tabs of white kersey, which fasten onto these buttons and serve to keep the swordbelt in place (Illus. 1401).

Pants, of deerskin [*losinnyya*] or, when unavailable, of goatskin leather worked like deerskin, are 37 1/2 inches long from the edge of the swordbelt, i.e. reaching to within 8 3/4 inches of the heels, and having a front panel [*latsbant*] covered by the coat's skirts.

Jackboots, with blunt toes, reaching to the kneecap, with applied bell tops, pieces over the spurs [*nadshporniki*], under the spurs [*podshporniki*], spur straps [*shpornye remni*], and iron spurs [*shpory*]; prescribed to be 21 inches tall from the heels, while the heels are 1 3/4 inches tall for men of all heights (Illus. 1401).

Riding trousers— of grey cloth and lined with black leather along the inner seam; they are prescribed to be 42 inches long from the top edge of the swordbelt, reaching to 4 1/2 inches from the heels, and having eighteen covered buttons along each of the side seams (Illus. 1401).

*Boots*for the riding trousers have rounded toes and short tops.

Neckcloth, with a small dicky, is made from black cloth backed with linen, and is tied in the back with small black ribbons. Its width and height are not regulated, and there is only the rule for the dicky that if a men has unbuttoned the top coat button and lifts his head, then the shirt must not be seen.

Forage cap— of white kersey, with band and trim the same color as the collar; it has the same pattern as forage caps in the infantry (Illus. 1401). Its height from the lower edge to where it folds over is prescribed to be 8 3/4 inches; distance from the fold to the tassel and tassel top — 10 1/2 inches; width of the round loop at the top of the tassel [*gaika*] — 1 1/4 inches; tassel — 2 1/2 inches; width of the band — 3 1/2 inches (Illus. 1401). The tassel is of two colors: white and the color of the collar. Tassel tops are according to squadron: in the 1st Squadron — white, in the 2nd — sky blue, in the 3rd — yellow, in the 4th — black, and in the 5th — green. In regard to hair style, care is taken that the front part of the hair (or *laverzhet*, as it is called) and the temples are cut smooth using a comb, while the back is gathered together into a thick, flat queue, intertwined with black wool tape so that the end of the hair is left out a little. Powder is only used in parades and on holidays.

Smock, of coarse calamanco, prescribed to be the same as in the previous tsar's reign.

Greatcoat— of undyed cloth, dark or light grey, only being the same shade for the whole regiment; with a similarly grey collar piped the same color as the coat collar, and with two tabs of that color— 1 3/4 inches wide and 2 5/8 inches long. A shoulder strap (on the left shoulder) is also the color of the coat collar; grey cuffs, round (Illus. 1402). It is made so that it can be worn not only over the coat, but also over the warm coat or sheepskin coat [*polushubok*]. In front it is fastened with seven buttons of the pattern and color as for the coat, sewn on and spaced one from the other so that when the swordbelt is worn over the greatcoat, the lowest button is under the swordbelt, while the upper half of the rear flaps come out above the swordbelt.

*Warm coat*or sheepskin coat is, as before, of sheepskin [*ovchinnaya*].

Hat, three cornered, bound with a black woollen cord; with a cockade of black worsted ribbon edged in orange; with a brass or tinned button, according to the coat buttons; with a cord around the crown and two tassels all of red wool, and a plume of white cock feathers. In front—11 1/2 inches, in back—12 1/4 inches, and between the corners and bottom edge of the crown—6 inches (Illus. 1403).

*Gloves*are chamois, with gauntlets (Illus. 1403).

Broadsword— with brass hilt; scabbard of unblackened leather, in iron mountings. It has a red Russian leather swordknot with a woollen tassel, left in the previous pattern as under EMPEROR PAUL I(Illus. 1403). As before, the color of the swordknot tassel is according to squadron: in the 1st Squadron — white, in the 2nd—sky blue, in the 3rd—yellow, in the 4th—black, and in the 5th—green.

Swordbelt, deerskin, as before, whitened, 2 inches wide, with welts at the edges, with two straps or slings 7/8 inch wide. With one large and two small brass buckles and with two brass rings, worn so that in front it covers the two bottom buttons of the coat, and in back its lower edge lies on the waist buttons (Illus. 1403).

Carbine— with brass fittings, with a strap of red lacquered Russian leather, and with a lock cover of the same material. The *crossbelt* is deerskin, whitened, 3 3/4 inches wide, with welts at the edges; for the carbine it has a brass buckle, cross piece, and end piece, with an iron hook; for the cartridge pouch it has two brass rings. *Cartridge pouch* (for 30 cartridges), of thick black leather, with the same brass plate on the cover as for infantry pouches, only smaller in size, and with two brass rings for the crossbelt. *Pistols* with brass mountings. All of these items remain the same as they were in the previous tsar's reign, with the only change being that the cartridge pouch is directed to be worn not over the right shoulder, but over the left, and not on its own strap, but on the same crossbelt used for the carbine, i.e. in that form which was used for dragoons under EMPEROR PAUL I (Illus. 1403).

Saddle, German, of black leather, with the holsters, saddle bucket, and other items of the same material; the stirrups and bridle and curb bits [*uzdechnyya i mundshtuchnyya udila*], of which the last has a raised image of a two-headed eagle, remain without the least change from those used in Cuirassier regiments under EMPEROR PAUL I.

Horse cloth[*popona*]of grey cloth.

*Shabrack*and*pistol holder covers* — cloth, of the same color as the collar, the latter being five-cornered and the first having rounded corners. These are trimmed around the edges with a cloth strip 1 3/4 inches wide, of the same color as the buttons. In both Life-Cuirassier regiments the shabracks and pistol holder covers have a worsted embroidered image of a black double-headed eagle on an orange field, surrounded by similarly embroidered white rays in the form of a star (Illus. 1403). The other Cuirassier regiments had the HIGHESTmonogram under the IMPERIAL crown, with a laurel wreath along the sides of this monogram, all cut out of cloth the same color as the buttons and sewn on (Illus. 1405).

Valise, of grey cloth, round, fastened with four brass buttons. Prescribed to be 23 1/2 inches long, 23 inches in circumference, 9 inches wide, and with a cover 16 1/2 inches long and 5 inches wide. [This cover refers to a flap over the valise - M.C.]

Forage sack, made of raven's duck.

Sack, of thick linen.

Water flask, wooden, wrapped or covered with leather.

Besides all these items, each squadron is issued with 16 tinned copper **kettles** with covers, the same number of **sickles** for gathering hay, 8 **axes**, and 8 iron **spades**. The last two items have leather cases and straps made from leather items and deerskin swordbelts and crossbelts that have passed their wearout time.

Cuirassier horse— no taller than 5 feet 3 inches, and not shorter than 5 feet. There is no prescribed color, but the cost, less delivery fee, is authorized to be 100 roubles.

Noncommissioned officers and first sergeants[*vakhmistry*] *of Cuirassier regiments*have the same uniform as cuirassier privates, but with gold and silver (according to the color of the buttons) galloon along the bottom (6) and side edges of the coat collar and on the cuffs, tassels on the hat that are white worsted with centers of orange and black, and the additional distinction of the top of the plume being of mixed orange and black feathers (Illus. 1404). Like infantry noncommissioned officers, they are authorized *stick canes [trosti]* which in mounted order are fastened, as before, to the butt of the right-hand pistol, putting the lower end through the horse's chest band. Of the arms and accouterments of cuirassier privates, they do not have the carbine and its crossbelt, and they wear the cartridge belt on a whitened deerskin crossbelt 2 5/8 inches wide, with welts at the edges, and no buckle, cross piece, or end piece. The tassels of their swordknots are white with a mix of black and orange, and their saddles do not have saddle buckets.

Distinguished officer candidates[*estandart-yunkera*] are uniformed and armed as noncommissioned officers, and have all the same horse furniture, except that the coat shoulder strap has gold or silver galloon (according to the color of the buttons) sewn down the whole length of its middle, and the saddle has a bucket for the standard [*shtandart*].

Trumpeters[*trubachi*] are uniformed as cuirassier privates, with a red plume instead of white. They are also distinguished from privates by wings or swallow's nests [*kryltsy ili naplechniki*] of the same color as the collar, and by trimming in the form of sewn-on woollen tape, 1 1/4 inches wide. In the Order Cuirassier Regiment this tape was of three black and two orange stripes, following the pattern for the ribbon of the Order of St. George (Illus. 1405). In the other Cuirassier regiments the tape is white with two stripes of the same color as the collar and, between them, similarly colored checks [in outline, not solid – M.C.] (Illus. 1406). Of cuirassier weapons, accouterments, and horse furniture, trumpeters do not have the carbine, carbine crossbelt, cartridge pouch, and saddle bucket. Trumpets [*truby*] remain the same as they were in the reign of EMPEROR PAUL I, with woollen tassels and cords of the colors of the coat's tape trim. This tape is sewn: along the round or lower edges of the swallow's nests and along the left front turnover of the coat — like buttonholes, doubled; on the swallow's nests — down the whole width, in three rows; on the upper halves of the length of the sleeves — over the whole width, in six rows, with the points upward; on all seams and along the turnbacks of the skirts — with the tape's whole width, while on the left turnover and on the cuffs — with doubled tape like a buttonhole (Illus. 1405).

Staff-trumpeter[*shtab-trubach*]— distinguished from the preceding squadron trumpeters in that, like noncommissioned officers, he has gold or silver galloon on the coat's collar and cuffs (according to the color of the buttons), a plume with a top of black and orange feathers, tassels on the hat and swordknot that are white with black and orange, and a cane (Illus. 1406).

The **kettledrummer**[*litavrshchik*] is uniformed and armed completely the same as the staff-trumpeter. *Kettledrums [litavry]* remain the same as used in the preceding reign. *Drum banners [zanavesy]*—of the same color as the collar, with embroidery and fringes in the color of the buttons—keep the previous pattern, except that the monogram of EMPEROR PAUL I is changed to that of EMPEROR ALEXANDER I.

When in full uniform and in formation, *officers*of *Cuirassier regiments* wear a cloth coat [*kolet*] of the same colors and cut as for cuirassier privates, but with white instead of colored piping at the sleeves' shoulder seams. *Pants* and *jackboots* were also like those of cuirassier privates; *spurs* are steel; instead of a neckcloth there is a black silk kerchief tied in back. Three-cornered *hat*, with the same decorations as in the infantry, but bigger, namely: in front — 10 1/2 inches; in back — 11 1/2 inches; and on the sides, from the crown to the edge — 6 inches. The feather plume is white, with black and orange at the base. *Gloves* are chamois, without gauntlets (Illus. 1408). A broadsword is prescibed to go along with this uniform, of the same pattern as the cuirassier privates', with a brass hilt, brass or iron (according to the color of the buttons) mountings on the scabbard, and with a swordknot whose strap is of black leather with silver thread stitching on the edges, while the tassel is flat, silver, with a fringe and a mix, in the middle, of black and orange silk. The *swordbelt* for this sword is the same as used by the privates, except that it is whitened under lacquer; it has buckles of the same color as the buttons. *Sashes [sharfy]* are exactly like those of infantry officers. *Cartridge pouches* are of black, lacquered leather, 8 inches long and 4 1/2 inches high, with two rings of the same color as the buttons. In both Life-Cuirassier regiments, pouches have a silver aureole in the form of an eight-pointed star, with a double-headed eagle in the center. In the Order Regiment, the pouch has gilt star of the Order of St. George, and in the rest of the regiments a stamped and forged (silver or gold, according to the color of the buttons) IMPERIAL monogram under a crown. These cartridge pouches are carried over the left shoulder on a whitened and lacquered deerskin strap 2 5/8 inches wide, with a buckle, cross piece, and end piece of the same color as the buttons (Illus. 1408, 1409, 1410, and 1411). *shabracks* and *pistol holder covers* are the same color—the first having pointed corners and the latter round ones, with gold or silver (according to the color of the buttons) galloon, and with embroidered designs: in the Life-Cuirassier regiments—stars, and in the rest—the monogram, as related above in the description of the shabracks and pistol holder covers for cuirassier privates (Illus. 1408 and 1410).

Generals[*Generaly*] are prescribed the same uniform, weapons, and horse furniture as officers, from whom they are distinguished only by white plumage on the hat (Illus. 1409).

While on campaign, instead of deerskin pants and jackboots, Generals and Cuirassier officers are prescribed to be in **riding trousers** of grey, semi-fine [*polutonkoe*] cloth, like those for cuirassiers, except with flat metal buttons in place of covered ones, in the same color as the coat buttons (Illus. 1409).

When off duty, Cuirassier Generals and officers wear a white cloth **undress coat** [*vitse-mundir*] lined with stamin of the same color, and with the same buttons, collar, and cuffs as on the dress coat. The undress coat has horizontal pocket flaps with three buttons, skirts with white cloth turnbacks that are edged with cloth of the same color as the cuffs and sewn down flat, with a gold or silver, according to the color of the buttons, aiguilette [*akselbant*] on the right shoulder. With this undress coat is worn a cavalry rapier [*shpaga*] identical to that used in EMPEROR PAUL I's reign, with an infantry swordknot, and carried on a swordbelt worn under the coat. shabracks and pistol holder covers with embroidery (according to the color of the buttons) are of the same pattern as was introduced in 1796-97 for officers' shabracks and pistol holder covers in Dragoon regiments (Illus. 1411).

*Noncombatants*have uniforms, accouterments, and weapons like those of noncombatants in the Army infantry, with the only difference being that their hats are a little bigger, as for combatant ranks.

The *manner of wearing the **hair and queue*** in Cuirassier regiments is exactly the same as in regiments of Army infantry (7).

In Cuirassier regiments the ***colors*** of collars, cuffs, shoulder straps, and the trim on skirt turnbacks, as well as of shabracks and pistol holder covers, are as follows:

In HIS MAJESTY'S Life-Cuirassier Regiment — sky blue; white buttons (Illus. 1401, 1402, 1403, and 1408).
In HER MAJESTY'S Life-Cuirassier Regiment — light raspberry; white buttons (Illus. 1404 and 1409)
In the Order Regiment— black, yellow buttons (Illus. 1405 and 1410).
In the Yekaterinoslavl Regiment— orange; white buttons (Illus. 1406 and 1411).
In the Little Russia Regiment— dark green; yellow buttons (Illus. 1406 and 1412).
In the Glukhov Regiment— blue [*sinii*]; white buttons (Illus. 1407 and 1412).

For everyday use, both while carrying out duties as well as when off duty, and also when on campaign, dark-green single-breasted cloth coats called ***surtouts*** [*sertuki*] are established for Generals and company and field-grade officers. These have similarly colored stamin linings, horizontal pockets, round cuffs, and turnbacks on the skirts — all dark green. The collar, shoulder straps, and trim or piping down the front, on the cuffs, on the turnbacks, and on the pocket flaps are all the same color as the dress coat collar. Buttons are flat (7/8 inch in diameter). These last are sewn onto: the front — 8, on the waist — 2, on the pockets — 3 each, on the shoulder strap — 1. Three more covered buttons are on the rear seams of the cuffs, to close them. In length and width these surtouts are prescribed to be the same as undress coats (Illus. 1412). While on campaign they are worn with riding trousers and boots with short tops, and during the rest of the time — with pants and jackboots. When carrying out duties, the broadsword is worn, belted over the surtout; when off duty, it is replaced by the rapier on a swordbelt worn under the surtout. (Illus. 1412).

18 October 1803— In Cuirassier regiments all combatant ranks, beginning with General Officers, are ordered to wear ***helmets*** [*kaski*], of black, lacquered *pompovyi* [? of unknown meaning - M.C.] leather, consisting of a round crown with visors in front and in back, two ear pieces on the sides, and a comb for a thick plume of hair, which is black for *privates* (Illus. 1413). For *noncommissioned officers* the plume is black with a white top that has one orange and two black stripes down the middle (Illus. 1413 and 1414); for *trumpeters* — red (Illus. 1414); for *staff-trumpeters* — red with the same top as for noncommissioned officers; for *officers* — white with a black top with an orange stripe next to it (Illus. 1415). The front of the helmet, starting from the top of the comb down to the visor, is decorated with a brass plate stamped with a double-headed eagle. The lower edge of the front visor is trimmed with a brass strip, doubled over. On the sides, over the ear pieces, are fixed two brass knobs, and on the inside are sewn (for covering the ears in winter weather) two cloth flaps, to which are tied leather straps, as for the infantry shakos established in 1803. At first, these straps were fastened over the flaps only in winter weather, but later this was done in any weather (9). In this same year, the **hats** prescribed for field and company-grade officers of Cuirassier regiments when not on duty are ordered to be of the pattern confirmed at this time for field and company-grade officers of the infantry, i.e. with a small button loop of narrow galloon and a high plume (10).

5 March 1805— Cuirassier regiments are ordered to have **pistols** that are shorter than before, being the same model as pistols throughout the cavalry (11).

1 July 1806— There is the same change in the uniforms of **regimental doctors** as described above for Grenadier regiments (12).

1 October 1806— **Warm coats** [*fufaiki*] are withdrawn from lower ranks in Cuirassier regiments (13).

2 December 1806— Lower ranks are ordered to cut off their **queues**, leaving their hair cut short under a comb. Regarding this, however, generals and field and company-grade officers are allowed to proceed according to their own wishes (14).

17 September 1807— Generals and field and company-grade officers of Cuirassier regiments are given **epaulettes** [*epolety*] patterned after those of the infantry and described above in detail for Grenadier regiments, but with a completely silver or gold field, according to the color of the buttons, and with cloth backing of the same color as the collar. On the kolet coat and the single-breasted coat, these epaulettes are prescribed to be worn on both shoulders, while on the undress coat [*vitse-mundir*] these are only worn on the left, leaving the aiguilette on the right (15). Around this same time **canes** are discontinued for officers and noncommissioned officers (16).

26 January 1808— During parades, or on officially listed holidays, and, in general, whenever troops are gathered, both in peace and in war, generals of Cuirassier regiments are ordered to wear the newly established standard **general-officer's uniform**, but when in **regimental uniform** and not on duty, they are to have dark-green pants instead of white (17).

Note: A description of the standard general-officer's uniform is found in a subsequent volume at the end of the overview of EMPEROR ALEXANDER I's reign, in the chapter about general officers' uniforms.

12 November 1808— On ordinary days [*budni*], Cuirassier Generals and officers in the surtout established in 1802 are allowed to wear **dark-green cloth pants** (18).

26 November 1808— All Cuirassier regiments are ordered to have new-style flat **plumes** on their helmets while on campaign. For officers, noncommissioned officers, and privates, these are black; for musicians — red. The previous chinstrap is replaced by new ones with flat brass **scales** (Illus. 1416 and 1417) (19). In this same year, long-skirted dark-green **frock coats** [*sertuki*] are introduced for officers of Cuirassier regiments, of the pattern described above for Army infantry. The collar (of velvet in the Order and Little Russia Regiments), cuffs, and buttons are according to the colors for the kolet coat (Illus. 1418). The previous surtouts introduced in 1802 now begin to be called dark-green **undress coats** [*vitse-mundiry*] (20).

11 February 1809— In place of their previous hats and forage caps with tassels, **noncombatant lower ranks** not holding noncommissioned officer rank are given new-pattern **caps** [*shapki*] identical to those which at this same time are introduced for Grenadier regiments, except that they are completely dark green with red piping around the edges of the band (21).

27 March 1809— The current **aiguilettes** on Cuirassier officers' undress coats are withdrawn, and subsequently undress coats are ordered to be worn with two epaulettes (22).

4 April 1809— **noncommissioned officers** are ordered to have galloon not on the bottom and side edges of the collar, but on the top and side edges (23).

8 June 1809— The plumage on **generals' hats** is discontinued and the former style of buttonhole loop is replaced by a new one, made of four thick twisted cords of which the two middle ones are intertwined in braid-like fashion (24).

13 August 1809— Instead of one **shoulder strap**, lower ranks in Cuirassier regiments are ordered to have two (25), and in this same year the **laurel wreaths** around the monograms on shabracks and pistol holder covers are abolished (26).

16 June 1810— **Carbines** and **pistols** for Cuirassier regiments are ordered to be made according to the newly confirmed patterns. Both of these, and infantry muskets, are of identical caliber (seven lines, measured in English inches [i.e. 0.7 inches - M.C.]), and along with this the first of these are prescribed to no longer be called carbines, but *cuirassier muskets* [*kirasirskiya ruzhya*] (27). In this same year, new-pattern **broadswords** [*palashi*] are introduced, with a brass hilt and full iron scabbard, without any leather (Illus. 1419). Also, the high **plumes** are shortened on the general's and officer's hat in use since 1804 (28).

16 September 1811— The rings on cuirassier **cartridge pouches** are taken away, and it is ordered that these pouches are to be worn in the fashion of infantry pouches, i.e. with the ends of the crossbelt put under the cartridge pouch (29).

23 September 1811— Lower ranks of Cuirassier regiments are given new-pattern **forage caps**, in the style of those established at this time in the infantry, except that they are white with the band and piping in the same color as the collar, and with the squadron number. Officers wear the same cap, but without a number and with a visor of black lacquered leather (30).

12 October 1811— The **newly established Cuirassier regiments**, *Astrakhan* and *Novgorod*, are prescribed the same uniforms as for other Cuirassier regiments: the first—with yellow as the distinctive color, and the second—with rose; both with white buttons and silver (Illus. 1419 and 1420) (31).

5 December 1811— The **kettledrummers** now in Cuirassier regiments are abolished (32).

17 December 1811— In place of the uniform they have had since 1802, **noncombatant lower ranks** are given a new one identical to that established at this time for noncombatant lower ranks in Grenadier and Musketeer regiments (33).

At the beginning of 1812— All ranks in Cuirassier regiments are ordered to have **collars** on coats and greatcoats lower than currently, fastened by little hooks (Illus. 1419 and 1420), and cuirassier privates and noncommissioned officers are given black, iron *cuirasses*, lined around the edges with red woollen cord and consisting of two halves: the front or chest piece and the back. To the latter of these, at the shoulders, are fixed two support straps with black iron fittings in the form of scales, with brass end pieces fastening to two small brass buttons fixed to the front half. (Illus. 1421). Officers receive the same cuirasses but with brass scales, while musicians are not authorized them at all. From this time on, the thick **plumage** on officers' helmets for parades is completely abolished, and officers of Cuirassier regiments are ordered to have **gloves with gauntlets** (34).

12 April 1812— Cuirassier regiments are ordered to have **shoulder straps** of the following colors:

1st Cuirassier Division: *in HIS MAJESTY'S Life-Cuirassiers* — sky blue; *HER MAJESTY'S Life-Cuirassiers* — light raspberry; *Astrakhan* — yellow.
2nd Cuirassier Division: *in the Yekaterinoslavl* — orange; *Military Order* — black; *Glukhov* — blue; *Little Russia* — dark green; *Novgorod* — rose (35).

10 November 1812— **Carbines** are withdrawn from all Cuirassier regiments, and subsequently the only firearms left are pistols and 16 rifles [*shtutsera*] in each squadron (Illus. 1422 and 1423) (36).

29 November 1812— In order to lessen their **expenses**, officers of Cuirassier regiments are allowed to have: instead of gold and silver fittings to the epaulettes — bronze, colored yellow or white according to the buttons; instead of silver sashes and swordknots — white ones, of linen [*iz beli*]; and also linen [*belelyi*] galloon and embroidery on shabracks and pistol holder covers: instead of gold — orange, and instead of silver — white (37).

17 December 1812— The **Cuirassier regiments renamed from Dragoons** are prescribed uniforms:

Pskov— with raspberry distinctions and yellow appointments (Illus. 1422).
Starodub— with sky-blue distinctions and yellow appointments (Illus. 1423) (40).

The first of these regiments, instead of black cuirasses, is left with the colored (brass and steel) ones it captured from the enemy in the Patriotic War of 1812 (41).

27 December 1812— The newly added squadrons to the establishments of Cuirassier regiments are ordered to have tassels and rings on their **swordknots**: 6th — red; 7th, Replacement [*Zapasnyi*] — white with a mixture of red (42).

3 April 1813— Officers of**HIS MAJESTY'S Life-Cuirassier Regiment** are ordered to have silver embroidered **lace bars** on their coat collars and cuffs, and lower ranks are ordered to have sewn-on tape [*bason*], white with red tracery (43).

Note: On 3 October 1813 HIS MAJESTY's Life-Cuirassiers, assigned to the Young Guard, adopted the title *Life-Guards Cuirassier Regiment*.

3 October 1813— Officers of the**Order and Little Russia Regiments** are ordered to have cloth collars on their **frock coats** instead of velvet: in the first — black as before; and in the last (in place of the former dark green) — green, with this same color also for officers' shabracks and pistol holder covers in this regiment (44).

7 December 1813— Officers of all Cuirassier regiments are ordered to have white linings to the **frock coat**, with collars of the same dark-green cloth as used for the frock itself, piped in the same color as the dress coat's collar, and which piping is also prescribed to be on the cuffs and pocket flaps (Illus. 1424) (45).

6 April 1814— The white double-breasted **undress coats** [*vitse-mundiry*] used by Cuirassier officers since 1802 is replaced by a single-breasted one with nine flat buttons, a collar closed with small hooks, and piping down the front in the same color as the collar (Illus. 1425). Along with this, the dark-green undress coats are also ordered to have nine buttons down the front, instead of eight (46).

20 May 1814— Officers as well as lower ranks, in all Cuirassier regiments, are given single-breasted **dress coats** [*kolety*] with nine buttons, in place of the double-breasted ones. These have piping—in the same color as the collar— down the front and around the bottom to the tails, and white piping on the collar (Illus. 1426) (47).

At this same time, the **campaign riding trousers** with buttons, used by officers since 1802, are replaced by new ones: grey as before, with two wide stripes [*lampasy*] and piping, both of the same color as the dress coat's collar, and without leather on the inner seams (Illus. 1426) (48).

19 August 1814— Similar **riding trousers**, except with leather on the seams, are given to lower ranks of Cuirassier regiments (Illus. 1427), while the deerskin pants and tall boots or jackboots are only left for parades (49).

15 September 1814— Each Cuirassier regiment is ordered to have 1120 **carbines** [*karabiny*] and 112 **rifles** [*shtutsera*]. In this same year a white band or ribbon is added to the **cockade** on officer's hats, and which is later replaced with a silver one (50).

16 December 1815— In Cuirassier regiments, **trumpeters** are to have grey horses, and other ranks — dark colors (51).

24 January 1816— **Scabbards** for officers' rapiers are ordered to be of black, lacquered leather (52).

21 September 1816— For carrying rifles when in formation, carabiniers of Cuirassier regiments are ordered to have **bandoliers** [*pantalery*] with hooks on which hang the rifles, as used at this time in Lancer and Horse-Jäger regiments (53).

24 December 1818— In Cuirassier regiments, the **scales on helmets** are ordered to be raised or convex, instead of flat, and of yellow brass as before (54). In this same year, the supporting **straps on cuirasses** are ordered to be longer than before (Illus. 1428 and 1429) (55).

17 April 1821— The **Pskov Cuirassier Regiment** is ordered to have rose collars, coat facings, and shabracks, with white buttons and silver, i.e. as previously for the **Novgorod Regiment**, while the Novgorod is to have raspberry, with yellow buttons and gold, i.e. as previously for the Pskov (56).

26 July 1821— The regiments of the 2nd and 3rd Cuirassier Divisions are ordered to have **horses** of the following colors:
Yekaterinoslavl and Order — light chestnuts [*svetlognedye*].
Glukhov and Starodub — sorrels [*ryzhie*].
Astrakhan and Little Russia — dark chestnuts and bays [*temno gnedye i karie*].
Pskov and Novgorod — blacks and dark browns [*voronye i temnoburye*] (57).

HER MAJESTY'S Life-Cuirassier Regiment, along with the Cavalier Guards, Life-Guards Horse, and Life-Guards Cuirassiers—making up the 1st Cuirassier Division assigned to the Guards Corps—have dark-chestnut, light-bay, and dark-brown horses (58).

29 March 1825—For faultless service, **chevrons** sewn on the left sleeve are established for combatant lower ranks: for 10 years of service — one; for 15 years — two; and for 20 — three, one over the other; all of yellow tape [*tesma*] (59).

II. DRAGOON REGIMENTS.

1 April 1801— **Dragoon regiments** are ordered to have:

a.) *In the Vladimir* — sky-blue cloth collars, lapels, and cuffs; yellow buttons and aiguilettes; for officers — gold lace-bars, with tassels (60).

b.) *In the Taganrog* — yellow cloth collars, lapels, and cuffs; yellow buttons and aiguilettes; for officers — gold lace-bars, with tassels (61).

c) *In the Narva* — sky-blue cloth collars, lapels, and cuffs; white buttons and aiguilettes; for officers — silver lace-bars, with tassels (62).

d)*In the Nizhnii-Novgorod* — black cloth collars, and cuffs; white buttons and aiguilettes; for officers — silver lace-bars, with tassels (63).

e.) *In the Irkutsk* — white cloth collars, and cuffs; yellow buttons and aiguilettes; for officers — gold lace-bars, without tassels (64).

f.)*In the Siberia* — white cloth collars, and cuffs; white buttons and aiguilettes; for officers — silver lace-bars, with tassels (65).

Based on this, the Vladimir, Taganrog, Narva, Irkutsk, and Siberia regiments receive the same uniform colors as they had since the beginning of EMPEROR PAUL I's reign through 3 April, 1800 (65), and the Nizhnii-Novgorod—since that same time through 29 May 1798 (67).

9 April 1801— Lower ranks are ordered to cut off their **curls** and have **queues** [*kosy*] only 7 inches [*4 vershka*] long, tying them at the middle of the collar (68).

27 February 1802— In place of their previous **gloves** with gauntlets, officers of Dragoon regiments are to have short gloves without gauntlets, of the pattern used at this time by infantry officers (69).

17 March 1802— Confirmation is given to the regulations for the cut, trim, and pattern of **Dragoon uniforms**, for combatant as well as for noncombatant ranks (70).

30 April 1802— Confirmation is given to a newtable of**uniforms, accouterments, and weapons** of Dragoon regiments. Based on this table and the previously mentioned regulations, *Dragoon privates* are prescribed: *caftan [kaftan]* or *coat [mundir], pants, boots, riding trousers, neckcloth, forage cap, smock, greatcoat, warm coat, hat, gloves, saber [sablya] with swordknot, sword belt, musketoon [mushket] with bayonet, sling, and lock cover, cartridge pouch with crossbelt and hook,* and, when in mounted formation, *a pair of pistols.* Horse furniture and accessories include: *saddle with saddle bucket, holsters, bridle, mouthpiece, cruppers, chestband, saddle girth, stirrups, cushion for the pack load, and small horse cloth; shabrack,pistol holder covers, valise. forage sack, bag,* and*water flask.*

The *caftan* or *coat* is prescribed to be double-breasted, of light-green cloth, with a standing collar that is of a particular color in each regiment, cuffs and shoulder strap (on the left shoulder) of the same color as the collar, with red linings to the skirts and tails, and with flat buttons—white or yellow in accordance with the particular instructions set forth below (Illus. 1430). This caftan, in winter as well as summer, is to be buttoned with all its buttons, and the sizes of its parts, assuming a man of 6 feet in height, are prescribed as follows:

Collar height, in front, at the edges — 3 1/2 inches, behind, at the middle — 4 inches; the upper edge shorter than the lower by 3 1/2 inches. Cuff width (slit) — 3 inches.

Length of the caftan, from the collar to the waist — 17 1/2 inches, and from the waist to the ends of the skirts — 12 1/4 inches; width of the front turnover — 3 inches; the distance of the first button from the collar — 1 inch; between the first and second buttons, and so on — 2 5/8 inches; between the buttonholes and the edges of the front turnover — 1/2 inch.

Lining on the skirts [*poly*] [before being turned back – M.C.]: on the straight [front] edge — 16 1/4 inches, on the other edge — 15 3/4 inches; top overlap [*nakos*] — 1/2 inch, below — 3 inches.

Lining on the skirts [*faldy*] [after being turned back – M.C.]: on the straight [front] edge — 11 3/4 inches, on the other edge — 11 1/4 inches; on the top end — 1/2 inch, on the bottom end — 3 inches.

Length of the shoulder strap — 5 2/3 inches, its width at the shoulder — 1 3/4 inches, width at the button — 1 1/4 inches.

Buttons are sewn on: on the right side of the front turnover — 7, on the left — 6, on the collar, for the shoulder strap — 1; on the cuffs — 2 each; on the waist — 2; at the joinings of the skirt and tail linings — 1 each.

Above the waist buttons, as on cuirassier coats, there are to be two cloth tabs, of the same color as the coat, to fasten onto these buttons and keep the swordbelt in place.

Pants, of white cloth, 37 1/2 inches long from the top edge of the swordbelt, i.e. reaching to within 8 3/4 inches of the heels, and having a front panel [*latsbant*] covered by the coat's skirts.

Boots for the pants, blacked [*smaznye*], with blunt toes, with screwed-on iron spurs. Prescribed to be 17 inches tall from the heels up, with a 2 1/4 inch cutout indentation in back, as in the infantry, and with 1 1/4 inch heels (Illus. 1430).

Riding trousers— of grey cloth and lined with black leather along the inner seam. With these are worn *boots* (blacked, round toed) and a neckcloth of black cloth, both prescribed to be the same as those established at this same time for cuirassiers (Illus. 1430).

Forage cap— of light-green cloth, with band and trim the same color as the collar; it has the same pattern, size, and colors for the tassels, and the round loop at the top of the tassel [*gaika*], as in Cuirassier regiments (Illus. 1430).

Smock, of coarse calamanco, *greatcoat*, of grey cloth, with collar, shoulder strap, and buttons, all the same colors as on the dress coat, and *warm coat* or sheepskin coat; *hat*, three-cornered, with plume of white feathers, and *gloves* with gauntlets; all the same size and pattern as described above for cuirassiers.

A *saber*, with steel scabbard, is prescribed for all Dragoon regiments, but from 22 June, in the same year of 1802, it is kept only for the regiments of the Kazan Inspectorate: the Vladimir, Nizhnii-Novgorod, Taganrog, and Narva. In all others it is replaced by broadswords of the previous pattern from the time of EMPEROR PAUL I(Illus. 1431).

*Swordbelt*for the saber, prescribed to be of the same pattern as established for Cuirassier regiments, with the addition of a small loop or frog between the two hanging straps or slings, for the bayonet scabbard. There is also a small leather strap with a small iron hook on which, in dismounted formation, the saber is fastened so as to be right up against the swordbelt. For regiments with broadswords, the swordbelt has a frog as used under EMPEROR PAUL I (Illus. 1431).

Musketoon, — with a bayonet, brass mountings; red strap and lock cover, and with a frizzen cover [*polunagalishche*] of Russian leather—remaining the same as previously.

Cartridge pouch, — with a brass plate, and attached to a *crossbelt* with buckle, cross piece, end piece, and hook— prescribed to be the same as for cuirassiers.

Saddle, — of black leather, with holsters, saddle bucket, and all other accessories being of the same material. An Hungarian pattern is introduced, of the pattern which was used by the entire Russian Regular cavalry from 1786 through 1796.

*Horse cloth*of grey cloth.

Saddlecloth [valtrap], — 44 1/2 inches long; 44 inches wide at the rear end, and 40 inches wide at the front— prescribed to be of cloth, the same color as the coat collar; with edging, monogram, and trim on the edges all yellow or white, according to the color of the buttons. The edging, 2 5/8 inches wide, is sewn on at a distance of 1/2 inch from the edge, while the trim goes along the very edge, so that on being bent over, 1/4 inch of it remains visible (Illus. 1431).

Valise, of grey cloth; *forage sack*, of raven's duck; *sack*, of thick linen, and *water flask*, wooden, wrapped with leather. All these are prescribed to be the same as for Cuirassier regiments.

Besides all these items, each squadron is issued 16 tinned copper *kettles* with covers, the same number of *sickles* for gathering hay, 15 *axes*, 8 *spades*, 4 *picks* and *mattocks*, with leather cases and straps for the last three items, made from leather items and deerskin swordbelts and crossbelts which have worn out.

Dragoon horse— no taller than 5 feet, and not shorter than 4 feet 10 inches. There are no prescribed colors, but the cost, less delivery fee, is authorized to be 50 roubles.

Noncommissioned officers and *first sergeants [vakhmistry]* of Dragoon regiments have the same uniform as dragoon privates, but with gold and silver galloon (according to the color of the buttons) along the bottom and side edges of the coat collar, tassels on the hat that are white worsted with centers of orange and black, and the additional distinction of the top of the plume being of mixed orange and black feathers (Illus. 1432). Like infantry and cuirassier noncommissioned officers, they are authorized *stick canes* which in mounted order are fastened, as before, to the butt of the right-hand pistol, putting the lower end through the horse's chest band. Of the arms and accouterments of dragoon privates, they are not authorized the musketoon, and their crossbelt for the cartridge pouch is only 2 5/8 inches wide, without a buckle, cross piece, end piece, or hook. The tassels of their swordknots are white with a mix of black and orange; swordbelts do not have bayonet frogs, and their saddles do not have saddle buckets.

Distinguished officer candidates *[fanen-yunkera, from the German "Fahnen-Junker"]* are uniformed and armed as noncommissioned officers and have all the same horse furniture, except that the coat's shoulder strap has gold or silver galloon (according to the color of the buttons) sewn down the whole length of its middle; their swordknots are of officer pattern (Illus. 1433), and the saddle has a bucket for the standard.

Note: Distinguished officer candidates [*fanen-yunkera*], as other noncommissioned officers, have cartridge pouches, but when they are in formation with a standard, these are not worn.

Trumpeters are uniformed the same as dragoon privates, with a red plume instead of white. They are also distinguished from privates by wings or swallows' nests of the same color as the coat, and by trimming in the form of sewn-on cotton tape, as for musicians in the Army infantry except more densely placed, namely: 5 rows on the wings, and 8 on the sleeves (Illus. 1434). Trumpeters have the same weapons, accouterments, and horse furniture as noncommissioned officers, with the exception of the cartridge pouch, which is not at all authorized for them. Trumpets remain the same as they were in the reign of EMPEROR PAUL I, with tassels and cords of white worsted.

Staff-trumpeter— distinguished from the preceding squadron trumpeters in that, like noncommissioned officers, he has: gold or silver galloon on the coat's collar and cuffs (according to the color of the buttons) (Illus. 1435); a plume with a top of black and orange feathers, tassels on the hat and swordknot—as well as tassels and cords on the trumpet—that are white with black and orange, and a cane.

Kettledrummer—uniformed and armed completely the same as a staff-trumpeter. *Kettledrums* remain the same as used in the preceding reign, and their *drum banners* remain the same color as the collar, with embroidery and fringes in the color of the button—keeping the previous pattern, except that the monogram of EMPEROR PAUL I is changed to that of EMPEROR ALEXANDER I (Illus. 1436).

Officers of Dragoon regiments are prescribed the same *coat* as privates, but with red stamin [*stamednaya*] lining, without shoulder straps or the seventh button on the right side of chest. It has horizontal pocket flaps with three buttons, with turnbacks that reach within a palm's breadth of the knee. In the Riga Dragoon Regiment the coat also has gold embroidered lace-bars on the collar and cuffs. When carrying out duties, officers wear: *deerskin pants; boots* with screwed-on spurs, of the pattern prescribed for lower ranks. Instead of a neckcloth, they wear a black silk *kerchief*, tied in back. *Hat, gloves, swordknot, swordbelt* (for the dress coat), and *sash* — all the same as for cuirassier officers, and a *saber* with a steel hilt (Illus. 1437). This last item, as mentioned above, was left only in the regiments of the Kazan Inspectorate, and replaced in all other regiments on 22 June, 1802, with the broadsword of EMPEROR PAUL I'S time, with the same swordbelt that was worn in that reign. *Horse furniture* remains the same as before, except for the saddle, which is replaced by an Hungarian pattern covered with a cloth *saddlecloth* of the same pattern, size, and color as described above for lower ranks, with gold or silver galloon and an embroidered monogram under a crown, according to the color of the buttons (Illus. 1438). Dragoon officers wear the same *greatcoats* as in the Army infantry and Cuirassiers, with a collar in the same color as that on the coat.

Generals, in regard to uniforms, weapons, and horse furniture, are prescribed the same as for officers, only with the addition of white plumage on the hat.

*While on **campaign***, instead of deerskin pants and the boots described above, Generals and Dragoon officers are to have riding trousers and boots with short tops, as in Cuirassier regiments.

*When **off duty***, Dragoon Generals and officers wear white *cloth pants.* Instead of the broadsword, they have a cavalry *rapier [shpaga]* with an infantry swordknot, and a swordbelt with frog, worn under the coat (Illus. 1439).

Noncombatants, both officers and lower ranks, are given the same uniforms, accouterments, and weapons as prescribed for noncombatants in Cuirassier regiments.

The *manner of wearing the **hair** and**queue*** in Dragoon regiments is exactly the same as in Cuirassier regiments (71).

In Dragoon regiments, the ***colors*** of the collars, cuffs, shoulder straps, and saddlecloths are as follows:
    In the *Riga Regiment* — red; yellow buttons (Illus. 1430).
    In the *Starodub Regiment* — red; white buttons (Illus. 1430).
    In the *Kharkov Regiment* — orange; yellow buttons (Illus. 1431).
    In the *Seversk Regiment* — orange; white buttons.
    In the *Tver Regiment* — blue [*sinii*]; yellow buttons (Illus. 1432).
    In the *Chernigov Regiment* — blue; white buttons.
    In the *St.-Petersburg Regiment* — rose; yellow buttons (Illus. 1433).
    In the *Moscow Regiment* — rose; white buttons.
    In the *Smolensk Regiment* — yellow; yellow buttons (Illus. 1434).
    In the *Kinburn Regiment* — yellow; white buttons.
    In the *Pskov Regiment* — flame colored [*ognevyi*]; yellow buttons (Illus. 1435).
    In the *Kargopol Regiment* — flame colored; white buttons.
    In the *Vladimir Regiment* — blanched [*planshevyi*]; yellow buttons (Illus. 1436).
    In the *Nizhnii-Novgorod Regiment* — blanched; white buttons.
    In the *Taganrog Regiment* — grey; yellow buttons (Illus. 1437).
    In the *Narva Regiment* — grey; white buttons.
    In the *Orenburg Regiment* — black; yellow buttons (Illus. 1438).
    In the *Ingermanland Regiment* — black; white buttons.
    In the *Irkutsk Regiment* — white; yellow buttons (Illus. 1439).
    In the *Siberia Regiment* — white; white buttons.
    In the *Kazan Regiment* — light raspberry; yellow buttons (Illus. 1439).
    In the *Kiev Regiment* — light raspberry; white buttons (72).

14 June 1803— In the **newly formed Dragoon regiments**—*Courland, New Russia, Borisoglebsk,* and *Pereyaslavl*—collars, cuffs, shoulder straps, and buttons are ordered to be of the following colors:

    In the *Courland Regiment* — turquoise collar, cuffs, and shoulder straps; yellow buttons (Illus. 1440).
    In the *New Russia Regiment* — turquoise collar, cuffs, and shoulder straps; white buttons.
    In the *Borisoglebsk Regiment* — violet collar, cuffs, and shoulder straps; yellow buttons.
    In the *Pereyaslavl Regiment* — violet collar, cuffs, and shoulder straps; white buttons (Illus. 1440) (73).

18 October 1803— In Dragoon regiments, all combatant ranks are given ***helmets*** in place of hats, of the same pattern as established at this time for Cuirassier regiments. Officers' hats are ordered to be worn only when off duty (74).

In 1804— Field and company-grade officers of Dragoon regiments are ordered to have **hats** of the same pattern as confirmed at this time for Cuirassier and Dragoon regiments, i.e. with a button loop of narrow galloon. These ranks, as well as Generals, are given high plumes, twice as big as before (75).

5 March 1805— Dragoon regiments are ordered to have **pistols** that are shorter than before, of the same model as pistols throughout the cavalry (76).

2 September 1805— For the **newly formed Dragoon regiments**: *Livonia* and*Zhitomir*, collars, cuffs, and shoulder straps are prescribed to be red with white piping, while buttons are: for the first — yellow (Illus. 1441), and for the second — white (77).

20 June 1806— In the newly formed *Finland* **and** *Mitau* **Dragoon Regiments**, collars, cuffs, and shoulder straps are prescribed to be white with red piping, while buttons are: in the first — yellow (Illus. 1442), in the second — white (78).

1 July 1806— There is the same change in the uniforms of **regimental doctors** as described above for Army infantry and Cuirassier regiments (79).

1 October 1806— **Warm coats** are withdrawn from lower ranks in Dragoon regiments (80).

2 December 1806— Lower ranks are ordered to cut off their **queues**, leaving their hair cut short under a comb. In this regard, however, generals and field and company-grade officers are allowed to proceed according to their own wishes (81).

16 December 1806— With their light-green coats, **newly formed Dragoon regiments** are ordered to have:
Tiraspol— light-green collar with red lining and scarlet piping; red cuffs and shoulder straps; yellow buttons (Illus. 1443).
Yamburg— light-green collar with red lining and scarlet piping; red cuffs and shoulder straps; white buttons.
Nezhin— light-green collar with turquoise lining; turquoise cuffs and shoulder straps; yellow buttons (Illus. 1444).
Arzamas— light-green collar with turquoise lining and piping; turquoise cuffs and shoulder straps; white buttons.
Serpukhov— light-green collar with yellow lining and piping; yellow cuffs, shoulder straps, and buttons (Illus. 1445).
Dorpat— light-green collar with yellow lining and piping; yellow cuffs and shoulder straps; white buttons.

In all these regiments, the greatcoat's shoulder straps and collar piping are prescribed to be the same color as on the coat (82).

These regiments, just as all other Dragoon regiments, except those in the Caucasus Inspectorate which have sabers (Vladimir, Nizhnii-Novgorod, Taganrog, Narva, and Borisoglebsk), receive new-pattern broadswords and swordbelts: the first item — with all-iron scabbards and brass hilts; and the second — with two slings, as for cuirassiers (Illus. 1442, 1443, 1444, 1445, and 1446). A new pattern of boot is also given, without a cut-out indentation in the back, and higher than before, up to under the knee (Illus. 1442, 1443, 1444, and 1445) (83).

17 September 1807— Generals and field and company-grade officers of Dragoon regiments are ordered to wear *epaulettes* on both shoulders, patterned after those described above for Cuirassier regiments, but in gold or silver according to the color of the buttons (Illus. 1446) (84). Around this same time **canes** are discontinued for officers and noncommissioned officers (85).

7 November 1807— In all Dragoon regiments, the light-green color of the **coat** is changed to dark green (86).

26 January 1808— When in parades, on holidays officially listed on the table, and, in general, whenever troops are gathered, both in peace and in war, generals of Dragoon regiments are ordered to wear the newly established standard **general-officer's uniform**, but when in regimental uniform and not on duty, they are to have dark-green pants instead of white (87).

21 February 1808— All Dragoon regiments are ordered to have **saddlecloths** [*valtrapy*] of a new pattern: dark green, with trim, piping, monogram, and crown in the same color as the collar (88).

12 November 1808— On ordinary days, Dragoon officers are allowed to wear **dark-green pants** (89). In this same year for these officers, there are introduced *surtouts* [*sertuki*] following the pattern confirmed for regiments of Army infantry and Cuirassiers, with a collar and cuffs of the same color as on the dress coat (90).

26 November 1808— Combatant lower ranks of Dragoon regiments are given **plumes** for their helmets of the new pattern confirmed at this same time for Cuirassier regiments (Illus. 1447). Officers are prescribed to have such plumes only when on campaign, and during the rest of the time their plumes are to remain of the previous style introduced on 18 October, 1803 (91).

11 February 1809— In place of their previous hats and forage caps with tassels, noncombatant lower ranks not holding noncommissioned officer rank are given new-pattern *caps* [*shapki*] identical to those which at this same time are introduced for Grenadier regiments, except that they are completely dark green with red piping around the edges of the band (92).

4 April 1809 — **noncommissioned officers** are ordered to have galloon sewn not on the bottom and side edges of the collar, but on the top and side edges (93).

8 April 1809— The slings [*pogonnye remni*] on **musketoons** are ordered to be of a new pattern, as established at this same time for muskets in the infantry (94).

8 June 1809— The plumage on **generals' hats** is discontinued and the former style of buttonhole loop is replaced by a new one, made of four thick twisted cords of which the two middle ones are intertwined in braid-like fashion (95).

13 August 1809— Instead of one **shoulder strap**, lower ranks in Dragoon regiments are ordered to have two (Illus. 1448) (96).

14 November 1809— Lower ranks of Dragoon regiments are ordered to have the skirts and tails of their **dress coats** shorter than before, like those of cuirassier kolet coats (Illus. 1448) (97).

16 June 1810— **Musketoons** and **pistols** for Dragoon regiments are ordered to be made according to the newly confirmed pattern. Both of these, and infantry muskets, are of identical caliber (seven lines, measured in English inches [i.e. 0.7 inches — M.C.]), and along with this the first of these are prescribed to no longer be called musketoons, but *Dragoon muskets [Dragunskiya ruzhya]* (98). In this same year the **plumes** on generals' and officers' hats are shortened (99).

16 September 1811— In Dragoon regiments, combatant lower ranks' buckles, cross pieces, and end pieces on the **belts** for the **cartridge pouch**, as well as the hook for the musket and the ring on the cartridge pouch, are all discontinued, while the cartridge pouches themselves are ordered to be worn in the manner of infantry pouches, i.e. passing the ends of the crossbelt underneath the cartridge pouch (Illus. 1448) (100).

23 September 1811— New-pattern **forage caps** are confirmed for lower ranks of Dragoon regiments, identical with those established at this time for Grenadier and Musketeer regiments, with the band in the same color as the coat collar and with the squadron number. Officers wear the same cap, but without a number and with a visor of black lacquered leather (101).

11 November 1811— The following Dragoon regiments are prescribed **colors**:

*Taganrog*and *Narva* — dark-green collar, with rose piping; rose cuffs and shoulder straps; rose piping, trim, and monogram on the saddlecloth; yellow buttons for the first regiment (Illus. 1448), and white for the second.

*Vladimir*and *Nizhnii-Novgorod*— dark-green collar, with white piping; white cuffs and shoulder straps; white piping, trim, and monogram on the saddlecloth; yellow buttons for the first regiment (Illus. 1449), and white for the second.

*Borisoglebsk*and *Pereyaslavl* — dark-green collar, with raspberry piping; raspberry cuffs and shoulder straps; raspberry piping, trim, and monogram on the saddlecloth; yellow buttons for the first regiment (Illus. 1450), and white for the second. (102).

5 December 1811— The **kettledrummers** in Dragoon regiments are discontinued (103).

11 December 1811— In place of the uniform they have had since 1802, **noncombatant lower ranks** are given a new one identical to that established at this time for noncombatant lower ranks in Grenadier and Musketeer regiments (104).

12 April 1812— Dragoon regiments are ordered to have **shoulder straps** of the following colors:
1st Cavalry Division: in the *Kazan* — light raspberry; *Riga* — red; *Nezhin* — turquoise; *Yamburg* — red.
2nd Cavalry Division: in the*Moscow* — rose; *Pskov* — flame colored; *Ingermanland* — black; *Kargopol* — flame colored.
3rd Cavalry Division: in the *Siberia* — white; *Orenburg* — black; *Irkutsk* — white; *Courland* — turquoise.
4th Cavalry Division: in the *Kharkov* — orange; *Kiev* — light raspberry; *Chernigov* — blue; *New Russia* — turquoise.
5th Cavalry Division: in the *Starodub* — red; *Tver* — blue; *Zhitomir* — red, with white piping; *Arzamas* — turquoise.
6th Cavalry Division: in the *St.-Petersburg* — rose; *Seversk* — orange; *Kinburn* — yellow; *Livonia* — red, with white piping.
7th Cavalry Division: in the *Smolensk* — yellow; *Pereyaslavl* — raspberry; *Tiraspol* — red; *Dorpat* — yellow.
8th Cavalry Division: in the *Vladimir* — white; *Taganrog* — rose; *Nizhnii-Novgorod* — white, *Serpukhov* — yellow.

Separate brigades: in the *Narva* — rose; *Borisoglebsk* — raspberry; *Finland* and *Mitau* — white, with red piping (105).

At almost this same time, **collars** on dress coats and greatcoats in Dragoon regiments are ordered to be worn lower than before, closed with small hooks (Illus. 1451), and the thick **plumage** on officers' helmets, prescribed for parades, is completely discontinued (106).

10 November 1812— **Muskets** are withdrawn from all Dragoon regiments, and subsequently the only firearms left are pistols, except for flankers (16 in each squadron), who receive **rifles** [*shtutsera*] (107).

29 November 1812— In order to lessen their **expenses**, officers of Dragoon regiments are allowed to have: instead of gold and silver appointments on their uniforms — bronze, colored yellow or white; instead of silver sashes and swordknots — white ones, of linen; and also linen galloon and embroidery on shabracks: instead of gold — orange, and instead of silver — white (108).

27 December 1812— The newly added squadrons to the establishments of Dragoon regiments are ordered to have tassels and rings on their **swordknots**: 6th — red; 7th Replacement [*Zapasnyi*] — white with a mixture of red (109).

20 May 1814— The **campaign riding trousers** with buttons, used by Dragoon officers since 1802, are replaced by new ones: grey as before, with two wide stripes and piping, of the same color as the dress coat's collar, and without leather on the inner seams (Illus. 1452) (110).

19 August 1814— Similar **riding trousers**, except with leather on the seams, are given to lower ranks of Dragoon regiments (Illus. 1453) (111).

30 August 1814— The Kiev Dragoon Regiment is ordered to have, on the **helmet plate** above the eagle, a brass shield with the inscription: "*Za otlichie*" ["For Excellence"], following the pattern for similar badges in the Army infantry (Illus. 1454) (112).

14 September 1814— Each Dragoon regiment is given 1120 **muskets**, separate from the 112 rifles in use since 1812 (113), and in this same year a white tape is added to the **cockade** on officers' hats, this later being changed to silver (114).

16 August 1815— The gold **lace-bars** on officers' coats in the Riga Dragoon Regiment, worn since 1802, are abolished (115).

16 December 1815— In Dragoon regiments, **trumpeters** are to have grey horses, and other ranks — dark colors (116).

1 February 1816— Dragoon regiments are to have the following **colors** for collars, cuffs, and buttons (117):
In the Kargopol — red collar and cuffs; white buttons (Illus. 1455).
— *Riga*— red collar and cuffs; yellow buttons.
— *Kazan*— raspberry collar and cuffs; yellow buttons (Illus. 1456).
— *Kiev*— raspberry collar and cuffs; white buttons.
— *Narva*— orange collar and cuffs; white buttons.
— *Kharkov*— orange collar and cuffs; yellow buttons.
— *Moscow*— rose collar and cuffs; white buttons (Illus. 1456).
— *St.-Petersburg*— rose collar and cuffs; yellow buttons.
— *Smolensk*— yellow collar and cuffs; yellow buttons (Illus. 1457).
— *Kinburn*— yellow collar and cuffs; white buttons.
— *Finland*— white collar and cuffs; yellow buttons (Illus. 1457).
— *Mitau*— white collar and cuffs; white buttons.
— *Ingermanland*— light-blue [*svetlosinii*] collar and cuffs; white buttons (Illus. 1458).
— *Tver*— light-blue collar and cuffs; yellow buttons.
— *Courland*— turquoise, or sky-blue [*goluboi*], collar and cuffs; yellow buttons (Illus. 1458).
— *New Russia*— turquoise, or sky-blue, collar and cuffs; white buttons.
— *Nizhnii-Novgorod*— brick collar and cuffs; white buttons (Illus. 1459).

18 September 1816 – Dragoons are given a new pattern of straight **spurs** (118).

28 Feburary 1817 – Officers of Dragoon regiments are ordered to have **cartridge pouches** of the pattern for Horse-Jägers, of black lacquered leather, with a silver cover decorated with a gold eagle, on a crossbelt trimmed with gold or silver galloon (according to the color of the buttons), with a silver belt plate and pair of prickers and chains (Illus. 1460) (118). In this same month all Dragoons are given a new **uniform** as follows:

1. **Shako** [*kiver*] of the pattern established on 17 September 1817 for Grenadier regiments, except with a red pompon [*repeek*], a white plume, and metallic appointments according to the color of the buttons (Illus. 1461). For privates, the base of the plume, and for non-commissioned officers the top, has black hair thinly mixed with orange; trumpeters and staff-trumpeters have the same plumes, but with red hair instead of white.

2. *Coat [mundir]*, single-breasted, of dark-green cloth, with nine buttons; collar and cuffs in the colors laid down on 1 February, 1816; trim on the skirts and piping the same color as the collar; two buttons on each cuff; coat lining of red kersey; epaulettes: yellow worsted when buttons are yellow, and white when buttons are white (Illus. 1461 and 1462).

3. *Riding trousers [reituzy]* of dark-green cloth, with broad stripes and piping the same color as the collar; with one button at the bottom, and with sewn-on boot cuffs [*kragi*] (Illus. 1461 and 1462).

4. *Saber [sablya]* and *swordbelt [portupeya]* with small hook; of the pattern used at this time in the Horse Artillery (Illus. 1461 and 1463).

5. *Gloves* (only for non-commissioned officers), short, without gauntlets (Illus. 1463).

Officers are prescribed the same uniform, with the usual distinctions differentiating them from lower ranks (120).

Regimental **colors** distinguishing the Dragoon regiments at this time are as follows:

1st Dragoon Division
In the Moscow — rose, white buttons (Illus. 1461).
— *Kargopol* — red, white buttons (Illus. 1461).
— *Kinburn* — yellow; white buttons (Illus. 1462).
— *New Russia* — sky blue; white buttons (Illus. 1462).

2nd Dragoon Division
In the Kazan — raspberry, yellow buttons (Illus. 1463).
— *Riga* — red, yellow buttons (Illus. 1464).
— *Tver* — light blue; yellow buttons (Illus. 1464).
— *Finland* — white; yellow buttons (Illus. 1464).

3rd Dragoon Division
In the St.-Petersburg — rose, yellow buttons (Illus. 1465).
— *Kharkov* — orange, yellow buttons (Illus. 1465).
— *Smolensk* — yellow; yellow buttons (Illus. 1466).
— *Courland* — sky blue; yellow buttons (Illus. 1467).

4th Dragoon Division
In the Ingermanland — light blue, white buttons (Illus. 1468).
— *Narva* — orange, white buttons (Illus. 1469).
— *Kiev* — raspberry; white buttons (Illus. 1469).
— *Mitau* — white; white buttons (Illus. 1470) (121).

14 March 1817— **Field and company-grade officers** of Dragoon regiments, when in formation with troops or when wearing sashes, are ordered to be in dress coats with short tails and wearing cartridge pouches (122).

16 April 1817— Dragoon regiments which have received **badges for distinction** [*znaki otlichiya*] are ordered to have them of the same pattern that is established for the infantry, i.e. in the form of a shield (123).

6 May 1817— **Trumpeters** of Dragoon regiments are ordered to have wings [*kryltsy*] on their coats in the same color as the collar (Illus. 1471) (124).

16 February 1819— For Dragoon regiments, when on campaign, ***covers*** *[chekhly]* are established for shakos and plumes, of raven's duck or Flemish linen, painted with black oil-paint, in the manner of oilskin (Illus. 1472), so that they do not allow water to pass through them. Detailed directives in this regard include the following:

"1. *About the shako cover:* the plume, cords, and pompon are removed from the shako (more is said below about the first item), and the remaining items are stored in the valise. The cover is put over the shako with visor, sewn to fit closely to it, with an overlap on the left side and fastening with small hooks. Over the cover, in the place where the pompon should be, is sewn a piece of cloth, of the same color as the pompon, and a shaped piece of wood is inserted here under the cover. In order to differentiate squadrons [*eskadrony*], squadron numbers in yellow cloth are sewn onto the front of the shako covers: in the first squadron a Cyrillic *1.E.*, in the second — *2.E.* and so on. The size of these numbers is 2 1/4 inches. To protect the rear of the soldier's head and his ears, there must be sewn onto the lower edge of the cover, in back, a piece of oilskin, painted on both sides, whose width is defined by the ends of the visor, and whose length by the height of the shako. In good weather this piece of oilskin in folded up and its side edges fastened to the shako cover with small hooks; in rainy weather, however, it is let down and in this manner protects the soldier from the wet."

"2. *About the cover for the plume:* the cover for the plume is to be 21 inches long, i.e. 1 3/4 inches longer than the plume itself, while its width is to be the same as the plume, and on both ends it has openings that can be tied and closed by small cords passed through it. Two leather loops are sewn onto this cover, lengthwise to the ends; the plume in its cover, with its upper end to the right and the loops underneath, is put into the valise on the horse, behind the saddle, and is held fast by two straps of this valise, passed through the above mentioned loops."

"3. *About cleaning the covers for the shako and plume:* these covers are to be cleaned with a brush, rubbing with a strong wax boot polish, so that they have a glossy luster; the cloth numbers and letters, though, are to be cleaned with ocher (125)."

20 February 1820— Shakos in Dragoon regiments, instead of hair **plumes**, are ordered to have small oblong woollen *plumes [sultanchiki]* or *pompons [pompony]*; yellow or white, according to the color of the buttons (gold or silver for officers) (Illus. 1473) (126).

18 April 1820— These **pompons** are discontinued (127).

7 August 1820— Generals who are assigned to Dragoon divisions, and field and company-grade officers of Dragoon regiments, are allowed to wear **moustaches** (128).

29 March 1825— Sewn-on **chevrons** on the left sleeve are established for combatant lower ranks who have rendered faultless service: for 10 years service — one, for 15 years — two, and for 20 years — three, one above the other; all of yellow tape (129).

At the end of EMPEROR ALEXANDER I'Sreign, it was ordered that **horses** be of the following colors in each regiment:

In the first regiments of each division (Moscow, Kazan, St.-Petersburg, and Ingermanland) — sorrels.

In the second regiments — (Kargopol, Riga, Kharkov, and Narva) — blacks.

In the third regiments — (Kinburn, Tver, Smolensk, and Kiev) — grey.

In the fourth regiments — (New Russia, Finland, Courland, and Mitau) — chestnuts(130).

The charge of Russian cuirassier at Borodino in the war of 1812

III. HORSE-JÄGER REGIMENTS

17 December 1812— The *Horse-Jäger regiments* renamed from Dragoons are ordered to have uniforms, weapons, and horse furnitureas follows:

Coat[mundir]— dark green, of the pattern of the current cuirassier kolet coats; with similar dark-green collars, with piping on the edges of the collar, shoulder straps, pointed cuffs, and with trim on the skirts and tails, all in each regiment's particular color, and with white buttons (Illus. 1474).

Pants[pantalony]— dark green, with wide stripes, piping, covered buttons at the bottom, and a cord for fastening these buttons, in the same color as the piping and cuffs on the coat (Illus. 1474).

Shako[kiver] — of the same pattern and shape as that used at this time in Grenadier regiments, except with a white metallic buttonloop and black cockade with orange edges, in place of a small grenade; with a green pompon — instead of red; with similar green cords — instead of white, and with a white plume, instead of black, with a black and orange bottom (Illus. 1474).

Saber[sabli]— of the pattern in use at this time by Hussars; with an iron hilt and scabbard fittings (Illus. 1474).

Swordbelt[pourtupeya]— of the pattern introduced a short time before in the Horse Artillery; with a small hook in front instead of a buckle (Illus. 1474).

Carbines[karabiny], **bandoliers** *[pantalery]*, **cartidge-pouch belts** *[lyadunochnyya perevyazi]*, **saddles** *[sedla]*, and *saddlecloths[valtrapy]* — following the patterns in use at this time in Lancer regiments; the last items being dark green, with trim and a monogram the same color as the piping and cuffs on the coat (Illus. 1474) (131).

Noncommissioned officers[unter-ofitsery] are distinguished by silver galloon on the collar and cuffs; by the swordknots, pompons, and shako-cord tassels prescribed for this rank in other regiments; by plume tops of black and orange, and by gloves. They do not have carbines or bandoliers (Illus. 1475 and 1476) (132).

Trumpeters[trubachi]— wearing the the same uniform as privates, they are distinguished from them by white chevrons on the coat and red plumes instead of white (Illus. 1477) (133).

Staff-trumpeters[shtab-trubachi]— compared with the preceding squadron trumpeters, these have the same distinctions as do noncommissioned officers compared to privates (Illus. 1478) (134).

Officers[ofitsery]— wearing the same colors and pattern of uniform as privates, they are distinguished from them, as in other regiments, by their pompons, shako cords, swordknots, sashes, and silver monograms and crowns on the saddlecloths. They have cartridge pouches that are the same as those given in 1817 to officers in Dragoon regiments (Illus. 1479 and 1480). Besides this they are authorized dark-green frock coats, with white buttons, and piping on the collar, cuffs, and pockets that is the same color as the piping on the dress coat (135).

The prescribed **colors** for piping, shoulder straps, cuffs, pants stripes, and trim on the saddlecloth are as follows:

In the Livonia Regiment— red (Illus. 1474).
— Pereyaslavl — raspberry (Illus. 1475).
— Seversk — orange (Illus. 1476).
— Dorpat — rose (Illus. 1477).
— Tiraspol — yellow (Illus. 1478).
— Chernigov — blue [*sinii*] (Illus. 1479).
— Arzamas — light blue [*svetlosinii*] (Illus. 1480) (Note: The same color as the collar in the L.-Gds. Semenovskii Regiment.)
— Nezhin — sky blue [*goluboi*] (Illus. 1480) (Note: The same color as the collar in the Courland Dra. Reg.) (136).

26 June 1814— Horse-Jäger regiments are ordered to have a single-breasted **coat** with nine buttons, piping down the front and over to the tails, the same color as the piping on the collar (Illus. 1481). In this same year, officers of these regiments are allowed to wear grey**riding trousers** for campaigns, with the same stripes and piping as on the pants (Illus. 1481) (137).

19 August 1814— Similar **riding trousers**, except with leather on the legs, are given to lower ranks of Horse-Jäger regiments, and the dark-green pants are kept for parades (138).

30 August 1814— The **Livonia Horse-Jäger Regiment** is awarded **badges** for the shako, inscribed *"Za Otlichie"*, in the shape of a ribbon and the same color as the helmet plate (Illus. 1482) (139).

In the same year of 1814, the **cockades** on officers' and lower ranks' shakos and on officers' hats are ordered to have a white ribbon around them, which is later changed to silver (Illus. 1482) (140).

1 February 1816— In Horse-Jäger regiments, it is ordered that cloth **tabs** [*klapany*] be sewn onto the collars of coats and frocks, of the same color as the piping and cuffs, with a white button at the end of each one (Illus. 1483) (141).

7 February 1816— In Horse-Jäger regiments, **piping** around the collar and down the front of the coat, **cuffs**, and **trim** on the pants, riding trousers, and saddlecloths, are to be as follows:

In the *Seversk* — orange (Illus. 1483), *Chernigov* — white (Illus. 1483), *Nezhin* — turquoise or sky blue (Illus. 1483), *Dorpat* — rose (Illus. 1484), *Pereyaslavl* — raspberry (Illus. 1485), *Livonia* — red (Illus. 1485), *Arzamas* — light blue (Illus. 1486), *Tiraspol* — yellow (Illus. 1486) (142).

12 July 1816— When not in formation with the troops, officers of Horse-Jäger regiments are allowed to wear **coats with long tails**, as in the infantry, but without horizontal flaps for the pockets (143).

16 July 1816— The monograms and crowns on the **saddlecloths** in Horse-Jäger regiments are to be trimmed with white cord (144).

18 September 1816— In Horse-Jäger regiments, **spurs** are ordered to be curved instead of straight (145).

8 March 1817— In Horse-Jäger regiments, the green **shako cords** are replaced with white ones (146).

17 March 1817— The **undress coat** [*vitse-mundir*] for Horse-Jäger officers, established on 12 July 1816, is to have dark-green trim on the skirts and tails, with piping of the same color as the cuffs (Illus. 1487) (147).

16 April 1817 — In Horse-Jäger regiments the **shako** is to have a plate of the same pattern as confirmed in this year for Dragoon regiments, and in the Livonia Regiment with a badge for distinction in the form of a shield (Illus. 1488) (148).

6 May 1817— **Trumpeters** in Horse-Jäger regiments are ordered to have wings on their coats of the same color as the shoulder straps (Illus. 1488) (149). In this same year, Horse Jägers are given new **sabers** and new **carbines** or, as they are called, *Horse-Jäger muskets*. The first have iron hilts and scabbards, and the second — bayonets (Illus. 1489) (150).

16 February 1819— Horse-Jäger regiments are to have **covers** for the shako and plume, identical with those established at this time for Dragoon regiments (151).

4 April 1819— In Horse-Jäger regiments the dark-green **pants** are ordered to have sewn-on cuffs of black leather, as for Dragoons (Illus. 1490) (152).

20 February 1820— Instead of hair plumes, the shakos of Horse-Jäger regiments are to have small oblong **plumes** or **pompons**: of white wool for lower ranks, and silver for officers (153).

20 April 1820— These **pompons** are abolished (154).

29 March 1825—For faultless service, **chevrons** sewn on the left sleeve are established for combatant lower ranks: for 10 years of service — one; for 15 years — two; and for 20 — three, one over the other; all of yellow tape (155).

At the end of EMPEROR ALEXANDER I's reign, it was ordered that **horses** in Horse-Jäger regiments be assigned by color:
    In the first regiments of each division (Seversk and Pereyaslavl) — sorrels.
    In the second regiments (Chernigov and His Highness the King of Württemberg's, formerly the Livonia) —blacks.
    In the third regiments (Nezhin and Arzamas) — grey.
    In the fourth regiments (Dorpat and Tiraspol) — chestnuts (156).

NOTES.

(1) *Complete Collection of Laws of the Russian Empire* [*Polnoe Sobranie Zakonov Russiiskoi Imperii*, hereafter PSZ — M.C.], Vol. XXVI, pg. 609, № 19,826.

(2) Archive of the Inspectorate Department of the War Ministry, in the book *Ukases of the Government Military College for the year 1801.*

(3) PSZ, Vol. XLIV, Pt. II, Section Four, Orders regarding uniforms, pg. 45, № 20,164.

(4) Ibid., pg. 45, № 20,186, and pg. 29, № 20,109.

(5) HIGHESTconfirmed table of uniform, accouterment, and weaponry items for a Cuirassier regiment, 30 April, 1802.

(6) PSZ, Vo. XLIV, Pt. II, in the Orders regarding uniforms, on pg. 74, line 12 from the bottom, as well as in the printed copies, distributed to the forces, of the regulations for clothing Cuirassiers at that time, it is stated that galloon is sewn *on the upper edge*, but according to all other sources, the testimony of contemporaries, and drawings preserved from that time, it is apparent that it was sewn *on the lower edge*, which was continued until 4 April, 1809.

(7) Everything stated here about clothing, weapons, and horse furniture for combatant and noncombatant ranks in Cuirassier regiments is based on: HIGHEST confirmed table of 30 April, 1802; rules located in PSZ, Vol. XLIV, Pt. II, Sect. IV, Orders regarding uniforms, pgs. 45-50, № 20,186, and pg. 29, № 20,109; drawings preserved in the SOVEREIGN EMPEROR'S Own Library in the Winter Palace, № 246 in the catalog; original articles preserved in various Arsenals, and the oral testimony of contemporaries.

(8) PSZ, Vol. XLIV, Pt. II, pg. 48, № 20,186.

(9) Ibid., Vol. XXVI, pg. 934, №№ 20,989 and 21, 191; drawings in the SOVEREIGN EMPEROR'S Own Library, № 361 in the catalog; actual helmets preserved in Arsenals; HIGHEST confirmed table of uniform, accouterment, and weaponry items of the Replacement half-squadron with a Cuirassier regiment, 17 December, 1803, and evidence from contemporaries.

(10) Evidence from contemporaries.

(11) PSZ, Vol. XXVIII, pg. 887, №21,651.

(12) Ibid., Vol. XLIV, Orders regarding uniforms, pg. 31, № 22,197.

(13) Information received from the Commissariat Department of the War Ministry.

(14) PSZ, Vol. XXIX, pg. 21, № 22,382.

(15) Ibid., Vol. XLIV, pg. 14, № 22,625.

(16) Evidence from contemporaries.

(17) PSZ, Vol. XXX, pg. 45, № 22,784.

(18) Information received from the Commissariat Department of the War Ministry.

(19) PSZ, Vol. XLIV, pg. 13, № 23,373; actual helmets preserved in Arsenals; drawings from that time and evidence from contemporaries.

(20) Evidence from contemporaries.

(21) PSZ, Vol. XXX, pg. 781, № 23,478, and model clothing preserved in the Commissariat Department of the War Ministry.

(22) HIGHEST directive declared to the Military College by the Minister of Military Land Forces.

(23) Information received from the Commissariat Department of the War Ministry, where there are also kept models of contemporary cuirassier clothing.

(24) PSZ, Vol. XXX, pg. 1006, № 23,695.

(25) Ibid., pg. 1096, № 23,690.

(26) Model shabrack, with pistol holster covers, preserved in the Commissariat Department of the War Ministry.

(27) PSZ, Vol. XXXI, pg. 215, № 24,263

(28) Evidence from contemporaries.

(29) PSZ, Vol. XLIV, Pt. II, pg. 54, № 24,774.

(30) Ibid., pg. 69, № 24,769, and evidence from contemporaries.

(31) Announcement of the Minister of War to HIS IMPERIAL HIGHNESS THE TSESAREVICH CONSTANTINE PAVLOVICH, 12 October, 1811, № 2588.

(32) PSZ, Vol. XXXI, pg. 910, № 24,899.

(33) Ibid., Vol. XLIV, Pt. II, pg. 31, №№24,911 and 24,912, and evidence from contemporaries.

(34) Evidence from contemporaries; contemporary portraits and drawings, and actual articles preserved in various Arsenals or held by private individuals.

(35) Archive of the Inspection Department of the War Ministry, in the book *Ukases of the Government Military College for the year 1812*, pg. 133.

(36) PSZ, Vol. XXXII, pg. 454, № 25,262.

(37) Ibid., Vol. XLIV, pg. 50, № 25,278, and model items kept by the Commissariat Department of the War Ministry.

(38) Ibid., № 25,292.

(39) Ibid.

(40) Ibid.

(41) Information received from the Inspection Department of the War Ministry.

(42) Information received from the Commissariat Department of the War Ministry.

(43) PSZ, Vol. XLIV, pg. 100, № 25,361.

(44) Ibid., pg. 133, № 25,463.

(45) Ibid., № 25,489, and evidence from contemporaries.

(46) Ibid., № 25,565.

(47) Ibid., № 25,589.

(48) Evidence from contemporaries.

(49) Ibid., Vol. XXXII, pg. 876, № 25,644, and evidence from contemporaries.

(50) Information received from the Artillery Department of the War Ministry, and evidence from contemporaries.

(51) Information received from the Inspection Department of the War Ministry.

(52) PSZ, Vol. XXXIII, pg. 1029, № 26,441.

(53) HIGHEST Order, and evidence from contemporaries.

(54) Model chin scales preserved at the Commissariat Department of the War Ministry.

(55) Evidence from contemporaries, and cuirasses preserved up to now in various Arsenals.

(56) Order of the Chief of the Main Staff of HIS IMPERIAL MAJESTY, 17 April, 1821, № 13.

(57) Order to the Cavalry of the Separate Corps of Military Settlements, 25 July, 1821, № 185.

(58) Information received from the THE HEIR AND TSESAREVICH'S Life-Cuirassier Regiment, 26 October, 1842, № 1278.

(59) PSZ, Vol. XL, pg. 188, № 30,309.

(60) HIGHEST Ukases announced by General-Adjutant Graf Liven to: the Vice-President of the Government Military College, General of Infantry Lamb — 1 April, and the Military College — 3 April, 1801. See also the entries for 29 May, 1798, and 3 April, 1800, in Volume VIII of *Historical Description of the Clothing and Weapons of the Russian Forces,* in the description of dragoon uniforms.

(61) Ibid.

(62) Ibid.

(63) Ibid.

(64) Ibid.

(65) Ibid.

(66) Ibid.

(67) Ibid.

(68) PSZ, Vol. XXIV, pg. 609, № 19,826.

(69) Ibid., Vol. XLIV, pg. 45, № 20,109.

(70) Ibid., pg. 51, № 20,186, and pg. 29, № 20,109.

(71) Everything stated here about clothing, weapons, and horse furniture for combatant and noncombatant ranks in Dragoon regiments is based on: HIGHEST confirmed table of 30 April, 1802; rules located cited in the foregoing Notes; drawings preserved in the SOVEREIGN EMPEROR'S Own Library in the Winter Palace, № 246 in the catalog; original articles preserved in various Arsenals, and the evidence of contemporaries. In regard to the *sabers* mentioned as part of the uniforms and weaponry of Dragoon regiments, information was received from the Artillery Department, and in addition based on the proposals of the Intendant-General of the Army to the Commissariat Commission, from 16 June and 4 July, 1802.

(72) PSZ, Vol. XLIV, pg. 52, № 20,186.

(73) Announcement by the Government Military College to the Commissariat Commission, 22 June, 1803.

(74) PSZ, Vol. XXVII, pg. 934, № 20,9989, and the same sources cited above in Note 9.

(75) Evidence from contemporaries, and actual hats from that time, preserved up to now in various Arsenals, including HIS IMPERIAL HIGHNESS'S Own Arsenal in St. Petersburg.

(76) PSZ, Vol. XXVIII, pg. 53, № 21,651.

(77) Ibid., Vol. XLIV, pg. 53, № 23,205.

(78) Ibid., № 22,185.

(79) Ibid., pg. 31, № 22,197.

(80) Information received from the Commissariat Department of the War Ministry.

(81) PSZ, Vol. XXIX, pg. 201, № 22,382.

(82) Ibid., Vol. XLIV, pg. 53, № 22,398.

(83) Information received from the Artillery and Commissariat Departments of the War Ministry; broadswords preserved in various Arsenals, including the one in St. Petersburg, and engraved illustrations of the uniform clothing and weapons of Dragoon regiments, in the SOVEREIGN EMPEROR'SOwn Library, catalog № 1.

(84) PSZ, Vol. XLIV, pg. 14, № 22,625.

(85) Evidence from contemporaries.

(86) PSZ, Vol. XLIV, pg. 54, № 22,877.

(87) Ibid., Vol. XXX, pg. 45, № 22,784.

(88) Ibid., Vol. XLIV, pg. 54, № 29,215.

(89) Information received from the Commissariat Department of the War Ministry.

(90) Evidence from contemporaries.

(91) PSZ, Vol. XLIV, pg. 54, № 29,378; the illustrations cited in Note 83; helmets preserved in various Arsenals, and evidence from contemporaries.

(92) PSZ, Vol. XXX, pg. 781, № 23,478, and model items of clothing kept by the Commissariat Department of the War Ministry.

(93) Information received from the Commissariat Department of the War Ministry. In general, models and illustrations of dragoon uniform items are preserved from that time: the first at the Commissariat Department of the War Ministry, and the second are cited above in Note 83.

(94) PSZ, Vol. XXX, pg. 950, № 23,625. See also this article in the preceding volume, under the description of uniforms and weapons for Grenadier regiments.

(95) PSZ, Vol. XXX, pg. 1006, № 23,695.

(96) Ibid., pg. 1096, № 23,790.

(97) Information received from the Commissariat Department of the War Ministry.

(98) PSZ, Vol. XXXI, pg. 215, № 24,263.

(99) Evidence from contemporaries.

(100) PSZ, Vol. XLIV, pg. 54, № 24,774.

(101) Information received from the Commissariat Department of the War Ministry.

(102) PSZ, Vol. XLIV, pg. 54, № 24,866.

(103) Ibid., Vol. XXXI, pg. 910, № 24,899.

(104) Ibid., Vol. XLIV, pg. 31, №№ 24,911 and 24,912, and information received from the Commissariat Department of the War Ministry.

(105) Archive of the Inspection Department of the War Ministry, in the book *Ukazy of the Military College for 1812*, pg. 133.

(106) Evidence from contemporaries, and information received from the Commissariat Department of the War Ministry.

(107) PSZ, Vol. XXXII, pg. 454, № 25,262.

(108) Ibid., Vol. XLIV, pg. 50, № 25,278.

(109) Information received from the Commissariat Department of the War Ministry.

(110) Ibid.

(111) Ibid.

(112) HIGHEST Order.

(113) Information received from the Artillery Department of the War Ministry.

(114) Information received from the Commissariat Department of the War Ministry, and evidence from contemporaries.

(115) Ibid.

(116) Ibid.

(117) PSZ, Vol. XLIV, pg. 134, № 26,111.

(118) Ibid., XXXIII, pg. 1026, № 26,436, and information received from the Commissariat Department of the War Ministry.

(119) Ibid., Vol. XLIV, pg. 101, № 26,727, and actual cartridge pouches preserved from that time.

(120) Ibid., sg. 134, № 26,728; actual models preserved by the Commissariat Department of the War Ministry; information received from this Department; engravings of Dragoons from that time, by Captain Kiel, now Major General of HIS IMPERIAL MAJESTY'S Suite, and evidence from contemporaries. See also the *Collection of Laws and Directives Relating to the Military Administration, for 1817*, book I, pg. 211.

[Ludwig Kiel (in Russian, *Lev Ivanovich Kil*) — At first he was an adjutant to Grand Duke Constantine Pavlovich, and then transferred to His Majesty's Suite. He painted watercolors and drew portraits on stone (for lithography), and then from 1815 to 1819 he engraved costumes of the Russian army at the request of Grand Duke Nicholas Pavlovich (later Tsar Nicholas I). At the end of the 1840's he lived in Rome and was the leader of the Russian artists' community there; he was an honorary corresponding member of the Academy of Artists. Died in Paris in November, 1851. Source: *Russian Biographical Dictionary.* - M.C.]

(121) See above, in the text for this volume, the entry for 1 February, 1816.

(122) PSZ, Vol. XLIV, pg. 101, № 26,727.

(123) Ibid., pg. 138, № 26,801.

(124) Information received from the Commissariat Department of the War Ministry.

(125) PSZ, Vol. XLIV, pg. 101, № 27,681.

(126) Ibid., pg. 134, № 28,153, and pompons preserved as artifacts and in drawings.

(127) Order of the the Chief of HIS IMPERIAL MAJESTYS Main Staff, 8 April, 1840 [sic, should be 18 April, 1820 - M.C.], № 21.

(128) PSZ, Vol. XXXVII, pg. 409, № 28,347.

(129) Ibid., Vol. XL, pg. 188, № 30,309.

(130) Evidence from contemporaries.

(131) PSZ, Vol. XLIV, pg. 58, № 25,292.

(132) Information received from the Commissariat and Artillery Departments of the War Ministry, and evidence from contemporaries.

(133) Ibid.

(134) Ibid.

(135) Ibid.

(136) PSZ, Vol. XLIV, pg. 58, № 25,292.

(137) Ibid., pg. 102, № 25,611, and model articles.

(138) Information received from the Commissariat Department of the War Ministry.

(139) HIGHEST Order and information received from this same Department.

(140) Information received from this same Department, and evidence from contemporaries.

(141) Information received from this same Department, and model horse-jäger uniform items preserved there. See also the illustrations of Maj. Gen. Kiel mentioned in Note 120.

(142) PSZ, Vol. XLIV, pg. 134, № 26,111.

(143) Information received from the Commissariat Department of the War Ministry.

(144) Ibid.

(145) PSZ, Vol. XXXIII, pg. 1026, № 26,434.

(146) Ibid., Vol. XLIV, pg. 136, № 26,722.

(147) Information received from the Commissariat Department of the War Ministry.

(148) PSZ, Vol. XLIV, pg. 138, № 26,801.

(149) Information received from the Commissariat Department of the War Ministry.

(150) Information received from the Artillery Department of the War Ministry, and actual horse-jäger sabers and muskets from that time. See also *Description of the Tula Arms Factory*, by G. Gamel, Moscow, 1826, pg. 442 and Table III.

(151) PSZ, Vol. XLIV, pg. 101, № 27,681.

(152) Information received from the Commissariat Department of the War Ministry.

(153) PSZ, Vol. XLIV, pg. 134, № 28,153.

(154) Order of the Chief of HIS IMPERIAL MAJESTY'S Main Staff, 18 April, 1820, №21.

(155) PSZ, Vol. XL, pg. 188, № 30,309.

(156) Evidence from contemporaries.

РИСУНКИ
ОДЕЖДЫ и ВООРУЖЕНІЯ
РОССІЙСКИХЪ
ВОЙСКЪ
1801-1825.

PLATES LIST OF ILLUSTRATIONS

1445. Private. Serpukhov Dragoon Regiment. 1806-1808.

1446. Field-grade Officer. Arzamas Dragoon Regiment. 1807-1811.

1447. Private. Serpukhov Dragoon Regiment. 1808-1811.

1448. Private. Taganrog Dragoon Regiment. 1811.

1449. Noncommissioned Officer. Vladimir Dragoon Regiment. 1811.

1450. Company-grade Officer. Borisoglebsk Dragoon Regiment. 1811.

1451. Company-grade Officer. Kinburn Dragoon Regiment. 1812-1814.

1452. Company-grade Officer. Kinburn Dragoon Regiment. 1814-1817.

1453. Noncommissioned Officer. St.-Petersburg Dragoon Regiment. 1817-1817.

1454. Helmet, Kiev Dragoon Regiment (with badge for distinction). 1814-1817.

1455. Private. Kargopol Dragoon Regiment. 1816-1817.

1456. Privates. Kazan, Narva, and Moscow Dragoon Regiments. 1816-1817.

1457. Noncommissioned Officers. Smolensk and Finland Dragoon Regiments. 1816-1817.

1458. Company-grade Officers. Ingermanland and Courland Dragoon Regiments. 1816-1817.

1459. Noncommissioned Officer. Nizhnii-Novgorod Dragoon Regiment. 1816-1817.

1460. Cartridge pouch for Dragoon Officers (established in 1817).

1461. Privates. Moscow and Kargopol Dragoon Regiments. 1817-1820.

1462. Privates. Kinburn and Little Russia Dragoon Regiments. 1817-1825.

1463. Noncommissioned Officer. Kazan Dragoon Regiment. 1817-1820.

1464. Privates. Riga, Tver, and Finland Dragoon Regiments. 1817-1825.

1465. Trumpeters. St.-Petersburg and Kharkov Dragoon Regiments. 1817.

1466. Trumpeter. Smolensk Dragoon Regiment. 1817.

1467. Staff-Trumpeter. Courland Dragoon Regiment. 1817.

1468. Company-grade Officer. Ingermanland Dragoon Regiment. 1817-1820.

1469. Field-grade Officers. Narva and Riga Dragoon Regiments. 1817-1820.

1470. Field-grade Officer. Mitau Dragoon Regiment. 1817-1825.

1471. Trumpeter. Mitau Dragoon Regiment. 1817-1825.

1472. Noncommissioned Officer. Mitau Dragoon Regiment. 1819-1825.

1473. Private. Mitau Dragoon Regiment. 1820.

1474. Privates. Livonia Horse-Jäger Regiment 1813-1814.

1475. Noncommissioned Officer. Pereyaslavl Horse-Jäger Regiment. 1813-1814.

1476. Noncommissioned Officer. Seversk Horse-Jäger Regiment. 1813-1814.

1477. Trumpeter. Dorpat Horse-Jäger Regiment. 1813-1814.

1478. Staff-Trumpeter. Tiraspol Horse-Jäger Regiment. 1813-1814.

1479. Company-grade Officers. Chernigov Horse-Jäger Regiment. 1813-1814.

1480. Field-grade Officer and Company-grade Officer. Arzamas and Nezhin Horse-Jäger Regiment. 1813-1814.

1481. Private and Company-grade Officer. Livonia Horse-Jäger Regiment. 1814.

1482. Horse-Jäger Shakos.

1483. Privates. Seversk, Chernigov, and Nezhin Horse-Jäger Regiments. 1816-1819.

1484. Private. Dorpat Horse-Jäger Regiment. 1816-1817.

1485. Noncommissioned Officers. Pereyaslavl and Livonia Horse-Jäger Regiments. 1816-1817.

1486. Field-grade Officer and Company-grade Officer. Arzamas and Tiraspol Horse-Jäger Regiments. 1816-1817.

1487. Company-grade Officer. Tiraspol Horse-Jäger Regiment. 1817-1825.

1488. Trumpeter. Livonia Horse-Jäger Regiment. 1817-1819.

1489. Horse-Jäger musket, confirmed in 1817.

1490. Private. Tiraspol Horse-Jäger Regiment. 1819-1820.

Privates. HIS MAJESTY'S Life-Cuirassier Regiment. 1802-1811.

Private. HIS MAJESTY'S Life-Cuirassier Regiment. 1802-1811.

Private. HIS MAJESTY'S Life-Cuirassier Regiment. 1802-1803.

Noncommissioned Officer. HER MAJESTY'S Life-Cuirassier Regiment. 1802-1803.

Trumpeter. Order Cuirassier Regiment. 1802-1803.

Staff-Trumpeters. Yekaterinoslavl and Little Russia Cuirassier Regiments. 1802-1803.

1407

Kettledrummer. Glukhov Cuirassier Regiment. 1802-1803.

1408

Officer. HIS MAJESTY'S Life-Cuirassier Regiment. 1802-1803.

1409

General. HER MAJESTY'S Life-Cuirassier Regiment. 1802-1803.

Officer. Order Cuirassier Regiment. 1802-1803.

Officers. Yekaterinoslavl Cuirassier Regiment. 1802-1803.

Officers. Little Russia and Glukhov Cuirassier Regiments. 1802-1803.

Cuirassier helmets from 1803 to 1808.

Noncommissioned Officer and Trumpeter. HIS MAJESTY'S Life-Cuirassier Regiment. 1803-1808.

Officer. HER MAJESTY'S Life-Cuirassier Regiment. 1803-1811.

1416

Cuirassier helmet of the Order Regiment, established in 1808.

Field-grade Officer. Order Cuirassier Regiment. 1808-1811.

Officers. HER MAJESTY'S Life-Cuirassier Regiment. 1808-1811.

1419

Noncommissioned Officer. Astrakhan Cuirassier Regiment. 1812-1814.

Company-grade Officer. Novgorod Cuirassier Regiment. 1812-1817.

Cuirass. Established in 1812.

Noncommissioned Officer and Private. Pskov Cuirassier Regiment. 1813-1814.

Private. Starodub Cuirassier Regiment. 1813-1814.

1424

General. Yekaterinoslavl Cuirassier Regiment. 1813-1814.

57

1425

Field-grade Officer. Yekaterinoslavl Cuirassier Regiment. 1814.

Company-grade Officer and Noncommissioned Officer. Order Cuirassier Regiment. 1814.

Private. Glukhov Cuirassier Regiment. 1814-1825.

Noncommissioned Officer. Yekaterinoslavl Cuirassier Regiment. 1818-1825.

Company-grade Officer and Staff-Trumpeter. Little Russia Cuirassier Regiment. 1818-1825.

Privates. Riga and Starodub Dragoon Regiments. 1802-1803

Private. Kharkov Dragoon Regiment. 1802-1803.

Noncommissioned Officer. Tver Dragoon Regiment. 1802-1803.

Fahnen -Junker. St.-Petersburg Dragoon Regiment. 1802-1803.

Trumpeter. Smolensk Dragoon Regiment. 1802-1803.

Staff-Trumpeter. Pskov Dragoon Regiment. 1802-1802.

Kettledrummer. Vladimir Dragoon Regiment. 1802-1803.

1437

Officer. Taganrog Dragoon Regiment. 1802-1803.

Officer. Orenburg Dragoon Regiment. 1802-1803.

Company-grade Officer. Kazan and Irkutsk Dragoon Regiments. 1802-1803.

Privates. Courland and Pereyaslavl Dragoon Regiments. 1803-1806.

Private. Livonia Dragoon Regiment. 1803-1806.

Private. Finland Dragoon Regiment. 1806-1808.

Private. Tiraspol Dragoon Regiment. 1806-1808.

Private. Nezhin Dragoon Regiment. 1806-1808.

Private. Serpukhov Dragoon Regiment. 1806-1808.

Field-grade Officer. Arzamas Dragoon Regiment. 1807-1811.

Private. Serpukhov Dragoon Regiment. 1808-1811.

Private. Taganrog Dragoon Regiment. 1811.

Noncommissioned Officer. Vladimir Dragoon Regiment. 1811.

Company-grade Officer. Borisoglebsk Dragoon Regiment. 1811.

Company-grade Officer. Kinburn Dragoon Regiment. 1812-1814.

Company-grade Officer. Kinburn Dragoon Regiment. 1814-1817.

Noncommissioned Officer. St.-Petersburg Dragoon Regiment. 1817-1817.

Helmet, Kiev Dragoon Regiment (with badge for distinction). 1814-1817.

Private. Kargopol Dragoon Regiment. 1816-1817.

Privates. Kazan, Narva, and Moscow Dragoon Regiments. 1816-1817.

Noncommissioned Officers. Smolensk and Finland Dragoon Regiments. 1816-1817.

Company-grade Officers. Ingermanland and Courland Dragoon Regiments. 1816-1817.

Noncommissioned Officer. Nizhnii-Novgorod Dragoon Regiment. 1816-1817.

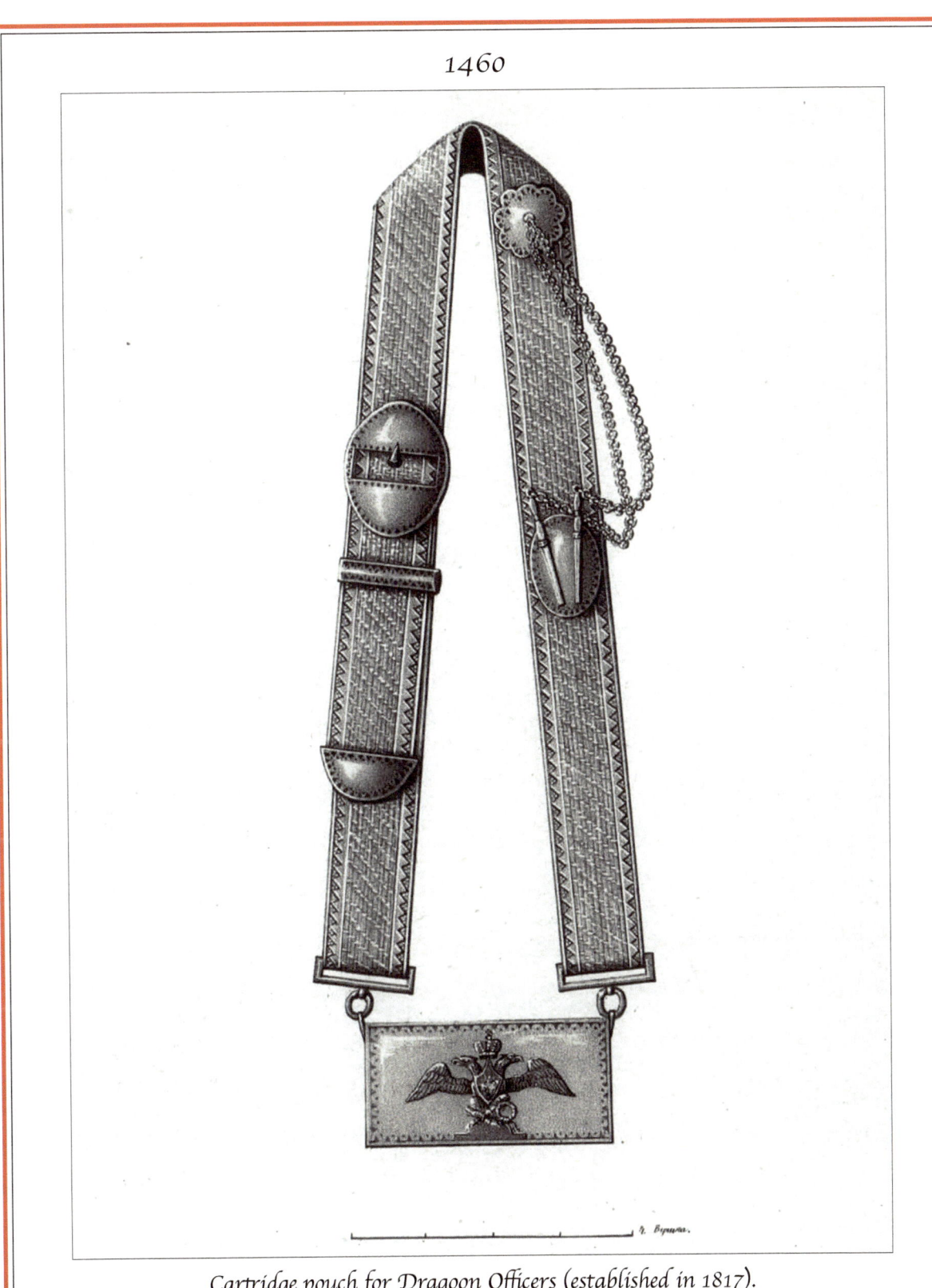

Cartridge pouch for Dragoon Officers (established in 1817).

Privates. Moscow and Kargopol Dragoon Regiments. 1817-1820.

Privates. Kinburn and Little Russia Dragoon Regiments. 1817-1825.

Noncommissioned Officer. Kazan Dragoon Regiment. 1817-1820.

Privates. Riga, Tver, and Finland Dragoon Regiments. 1817-1825.

Trumpeters. St.-Petersburg and Kharkov Dragoon Regiments. 1817.

1466

Trumpeter. Smolensk Dragoon Regiment. 1817.

Staff-Trumpeter. Courland Dragoon Regiment. 1817.

Company-grade Officer. Ingermanland Dragoon Regiment. 1817-1820.

Field-grade Officers. Narva and Riga Dragoon Regiments. 1817-1820.

Field-grade Officer. Mitau Dragoon Regiment. 1817-1825.

1471

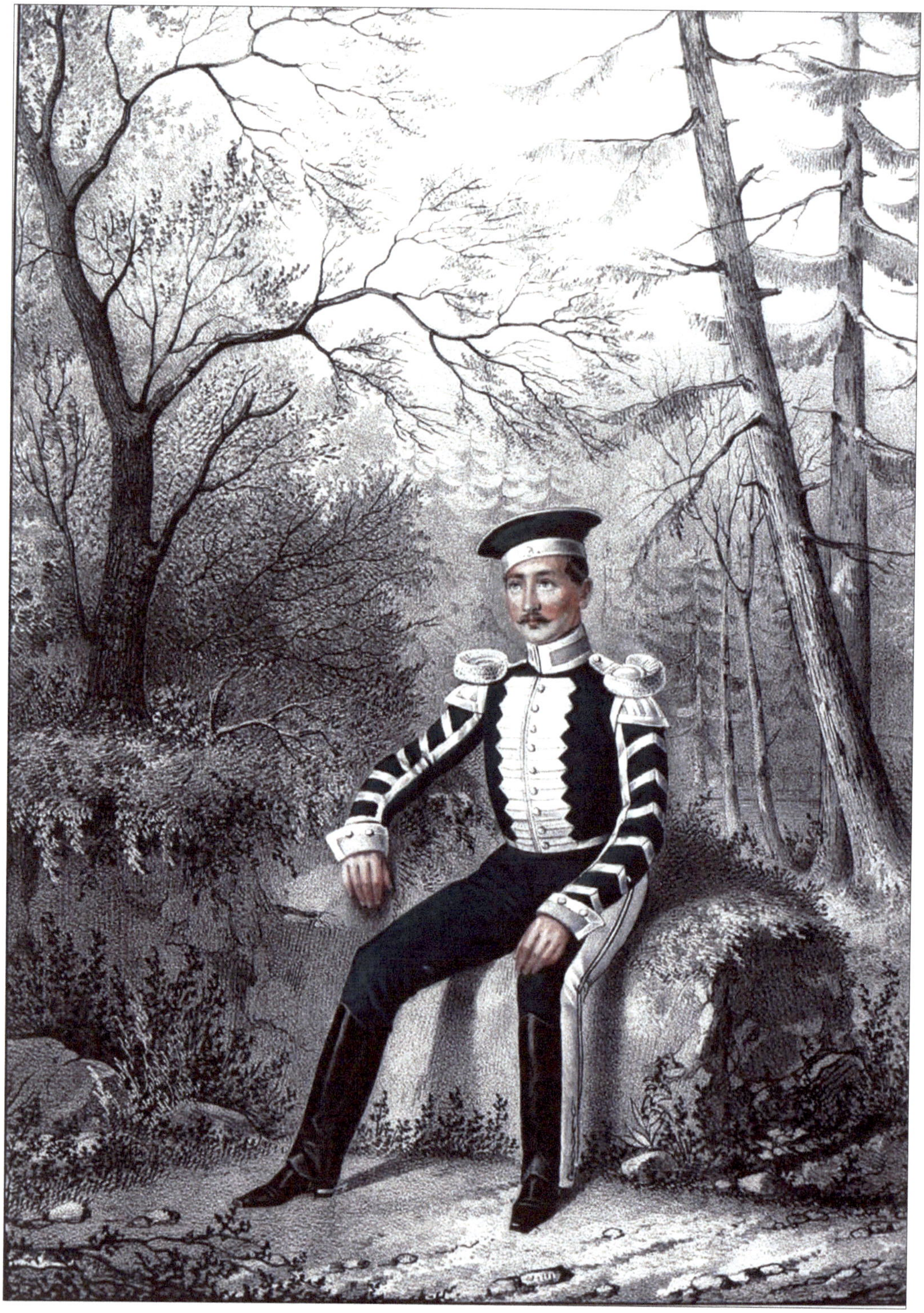

Trumpeter. Mitau Dragoon Regiment. 1817-1825.

Noncommissioned Officer. Mitau Dragoon Regiment. 1819-1825.

Private. Mitau Dragoon Regiment. 1820.

1474

Privates. Livonia Horse-Jäger Regiment 1813-1814.

1475

Noncommissioned Officer. Pereyaslavl Horse-Jäger Regiment. 1813-1814.

Noncommissioned Officer. Seversk Horse-Jäger Regiment. 1813-1814.

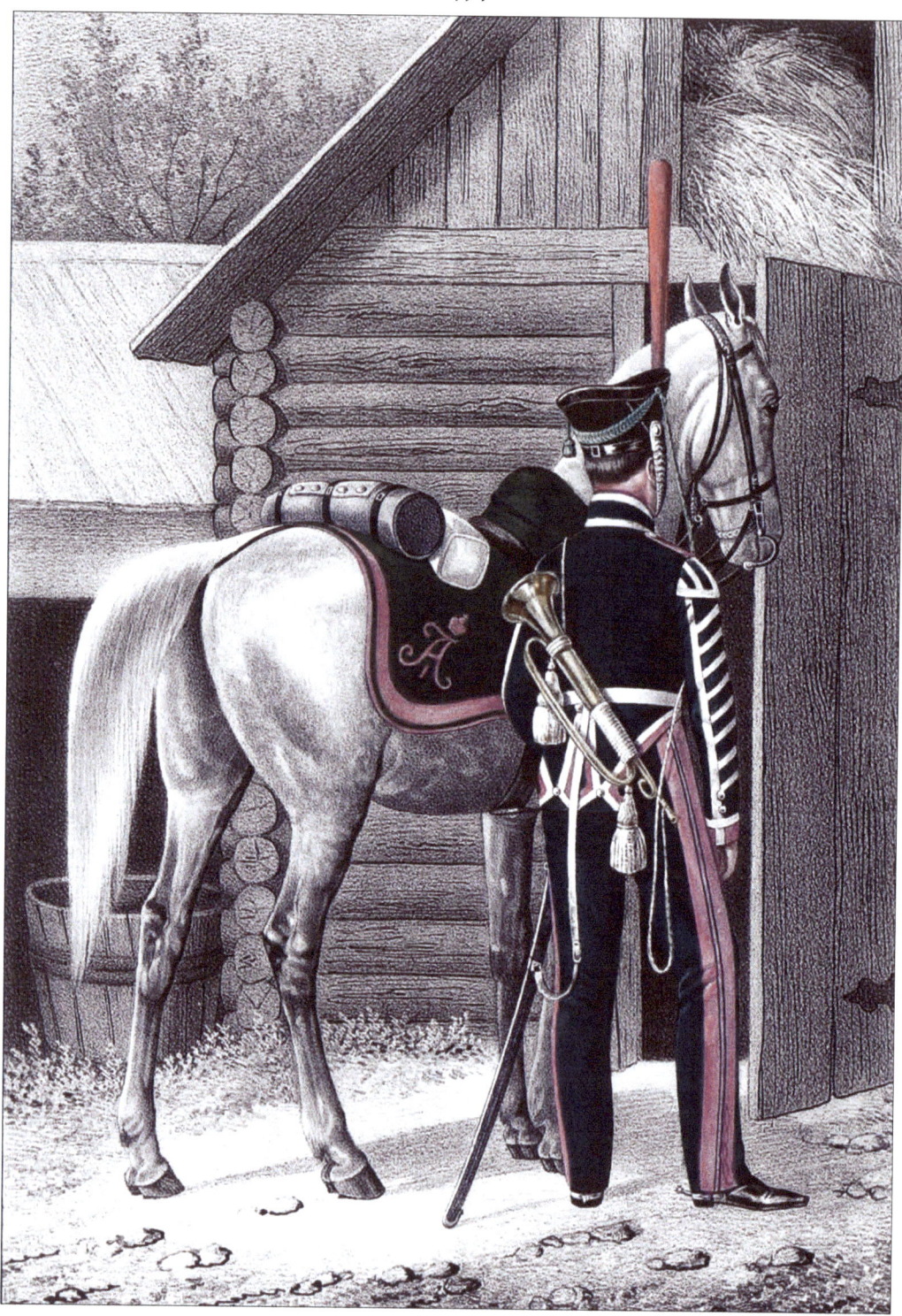

1477

Trumpeter. Dorpat Horse-Jäger Regiment. 1813-1814.

Staff-Trumpeter. Tiraspol Horse-Jäger Regiment. 1813-1814.

Company-grade Officers. Chernigov Horse-Jäger Regiment. 1813-1814

Field-grade Officer and Com. grade Officer. Arzamas and Nezhin Horse-Jäger Regi. 1813-1814.

Private and Company-grade Officer. Livonia Horse-Jäger Regiment. 1814.

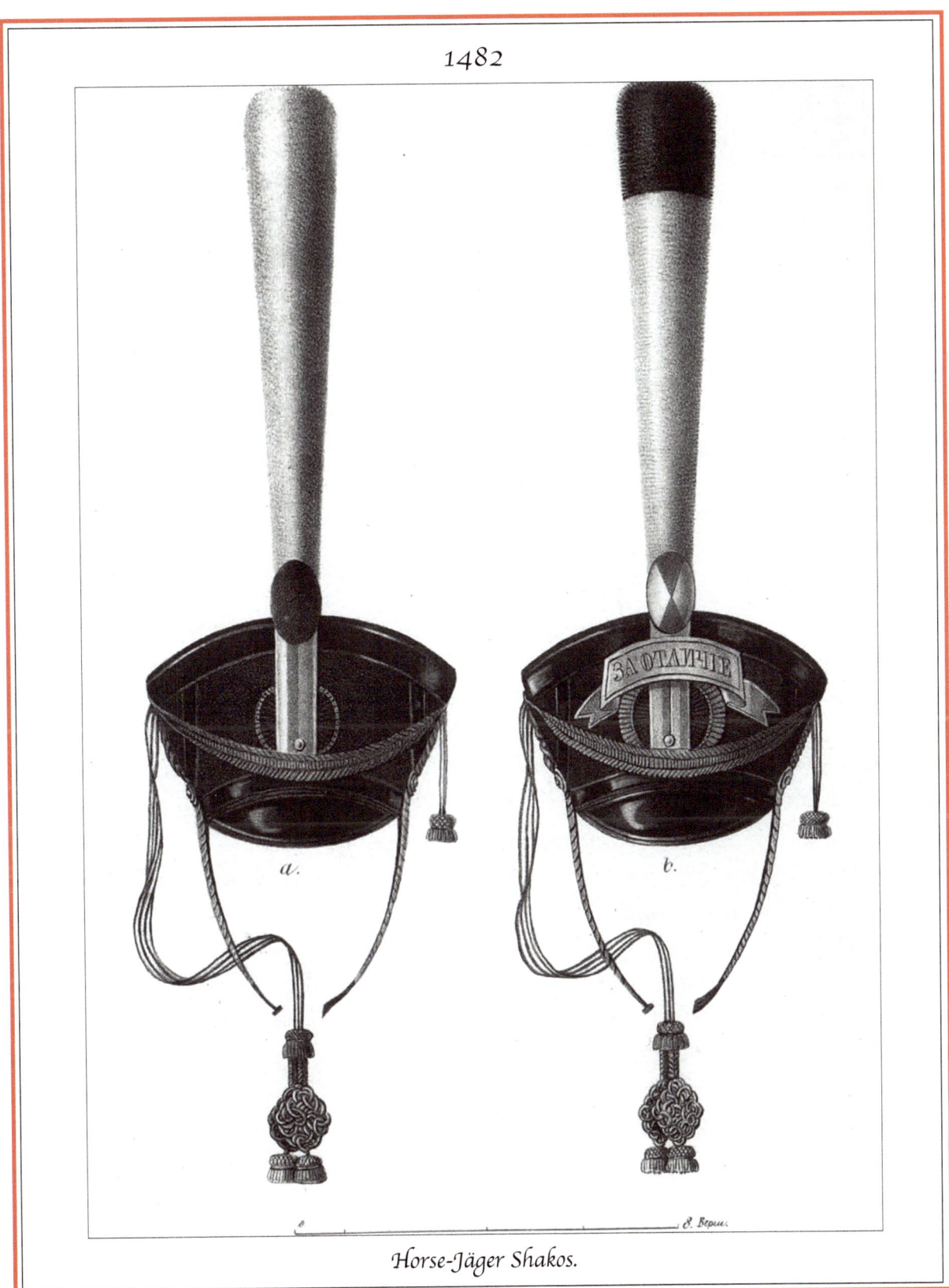

Horse-Jäger Shakos.

Privates. Seversk, Chernigov, and Nezhin Horse-Jäger Regiments. 1816-1819

Private. Dorpat Horse-Jäger Regiment. 1816-1817.

Noncommissioned Officers. Pereyaslavl and Livonia Horse-Jäger Regiments. 1816-1817

Field-grade Officer and Com.grade Officer. Arzamas and Tiraspol Horse-Jäger Reg. 1816-1817.

1487

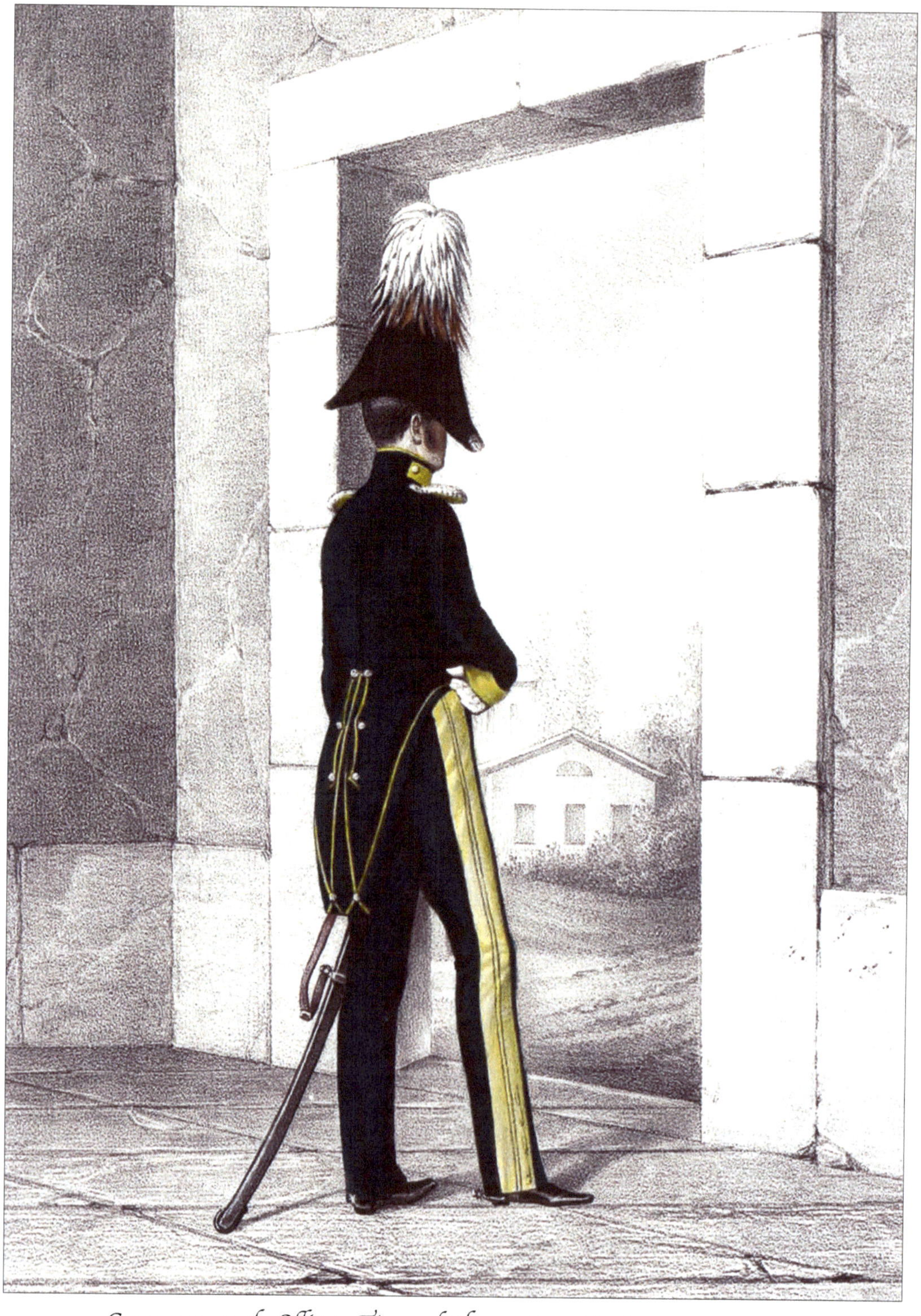

Company-grade Officer. Tiraspol Horse-Jäger Regiment. 1817-1825

Trumpeter. Livonia Horse-Jäger Regiment. 1817-1819.

Horse-Jäger musket, confirmed in 1817

Private. Tiraspol Horse-Jäger Regiment. 1819-1820.

SOLDIERS, WEAPONS & UNIFORMS ALREADY PUBLISHED
(TITLES ALREADY PUBLISHED)

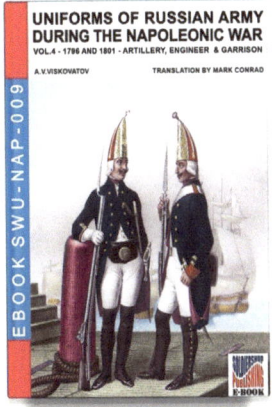

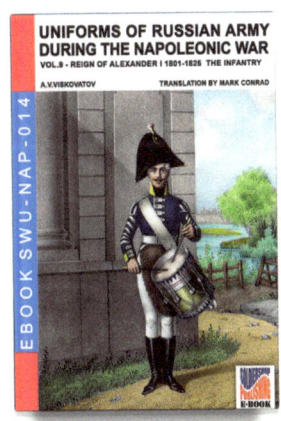

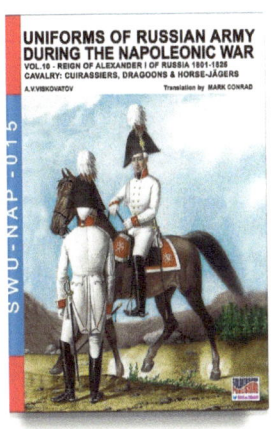

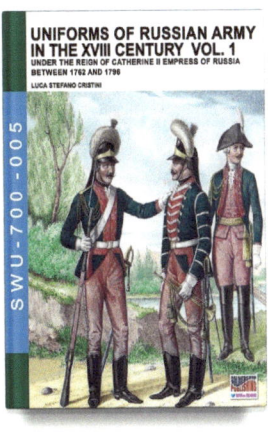

www.ingramcontent.com/pod-product-compliance
Lightning Source LLC
Chambersburg PA
CBHW041454120626
46547CB00003B/439